MORE BOOKS FROM THE SAGER GROUP

The Swamp: Deceit and Corruption in the CIA
An Elizabeth Petrov Thriller (Book 1)
by Jeff Grant

Chains of Nobility: Brotherhood of the Mamluks (Book 1-3)
by Brad Graft

Meeting Mozart: A Novel Drawn from the Secret Diaries of
Lorenzo Da Ponte
by Howard Jay Smith

Death Came Swiftly: A Novel About the Tay Bridge Disaster of 1879
by Bill Abrams

A Boy and His Dog in Hell: And Other Stories
by Mike Sager

The Deadliest Man Alive: Count Dante, The Mob
and the War for American Martial Arts
by Benji Feldheim

The Orphan's Daughter: A Novel
by Jan Cherubin

Lifeboat No. 8: Surviving the Titanic
by Elizabeth Kaye

The Pope of Pot: And Other True Stories of Marijuana
and Related High Jinks
by Mike Sager

See our entire library at TheSagerGroup.net

JACK MOVES

A MEMOIR OF THE WEED TRADE AND DANGEROUS LIVING

JEREMY NORRIE

Jack Moves: A Memoir of the Weed Trade and Dangerous Living

Copyright © 2022 Jeremy Norrie

Published in the United States of America.

Cover and Interior Designed by Siori Kitajima, PatternBased.com

Cataloging-in-Publication data for this book is available from the Library of Congress

ISBN-13:
eBook: 978-1-958861-03-5
Paperback: 978-1-958861-04-2

Published by The Sager Group LLC
(TheSagerGroup.net)

Jack Moves

A MEMOIR OF
THE WEED TRADE AND
DANGEROUS LIVING

JEREMY NORRIE

THE SAGER GROUP

Artifex Te Adiuva

Jackmove:
A slang term used in the 1990s to mean robbery.

Marijuana is NOT DANGEROUS. The risks people take to grow and sell it (even just to possess it) ARE DANGEROUS. The VAST MAJORITY of people hurt by marijuana are victims of CRIME or ARREST, not CONSUMPTION. MARIJUANA IS NOT DANGEROUS, THE PROHIBITION OF MARIJUANA IS. — Jeremy Norrie

CONTENTS

PREFACE

I used to do well in English classes when I was at school. I also really enjoyed them. However, I knew that nothing I'd write would ever measure up to the gilded hardbacks of the literary greats or the novels that most people enjoy today.

When it came time for me to start trying to find my place in the world, I decided to write, but in my own way. No, my writing wouldn't be on a shelf with world-renowned authors, but it would have substance, and it would resonate with people. At first, I was blogging, telling stories and anecdotes on platforms like Myspace. Before that, I also used Friendster and other sites, most of which were fighting or cannabis related.

I suppose I should explain this a little more. I am a huge fan of mixed martial arts (MMA). Most people know it as Ultimate Fighting or UFC. It has gone from being almost completely unknown to one of the most popular sports organizations today. When I first started out, I was doing a good deal of leisure writing on sites that focused on the sport, because many of the mainstream news sources totally ignored it. Sherdog.com and the Underground on MMA.tv were two of the biggest sites around at the time, and that's where I mostly wrote. I was contacted by a guy from one of these platforms, and he offered me the opportunity to write for a new website that he was working on. He gave me a weekly column, and I wrote for them for about a year.

That website was MMAWeekly.com, and that man was Ryan Bennett: a former UFC employee and a wonderful man in general. Everything was going great at MMAWeekly, but soon enough, they started to increase in popularity, and they moved on to other professional journalists, so unfortunately, I was not able to continue with them. Shortly after I left, Ryan was killed in a car accident at the young age of 35. This really was an eye-opener. Life can be over in the blink of an eye, so we should all be careful and live it to the fullest.

I then wrote for another small website called MMA-Fighter. During this time, I was periodically emailing Bruce Buffer, who eventually helped me get on the UFC street team. We attended the shows as media, and I even got paid by the UFC to promote one of their shows. For the most part, however, it was a good deal of work for not much in return.

I then began cannabis journalism. Although I had been doing all of these other things, the reality of the situation was that cannabis was paying my bills. I was often torn as to the value of my interest in this wonderful plant: Was it positive or negative for my life? Dozens of people told me I should leave cannabis behind me, that it was a childish drug, and that I should set my sights on new horizons.

I had an epiphany one night when I was contemplating my options. I was a very troubled and unhappy child in many ways, and I had been thinking about what would make me truly happy.

I realized that what is most important is noticing what makes you smile — not what you wish made you smile, but rather the things we can't help but smile at.

These are the things that knit your personality together. They form the core of your identity. These are the things you honestly love, not just because society tells you that you should. To follow your smile is to follow your heart. Nourish your mind with what it truly enjoys, and you'll find inner strength.

You must never let anyone separate you from these things. If you do like something, then maybe it's worth exploring. This exploration could lead you to experiences that you'll cherish for the rest of your life. It could also lead you to people similar to you, or to places where you'll feel at home and loved.

I enjoy cannabis, and the things related to its culture also provide me with great pleasure. Cannabis is medicinal to me, and it gives me the opportunity to enjoy life like a normal person. Being a part of this culture has allowed me to meet kindred spirits who share a similar mindset. Once I acknowledged that cannabis benefited me in so many ways, I was able to fully embrace it.

In one of my posts on Overgrow.com, I discussed California's medical marijuana laws, the effectiveness of vaporization and the different tools that are best used for that purpose. A man named Marco Renda read this post and invited me to write for his magazine, Treating Yourself, which focused on medical marijuana. He began by asking me to send him an article, and the rest was history. This was the first time that my writing had been published in print, and I wrote an article for just about every issue until the magazine ceased publication in 2013. The magazine was incredibly successful and well respected. Even today, it is considered one of the best cannabis magazines that ever was. Thanks to this experience, I have traveled the world writing articles, enjoying cannabis and meeting new people.

This all sounds very exciting, but it's worth noting that I didn't get paid for this. Everything I was doing came out of my own pocket, with some small perks here and there. Helping people who needed cannabis in general was still providing me with the lifestyle I had become accustomed to. Regardless of the other non-cannabis-related directions I tried to steer myself toward, I was always pulled back into marijuana. I viewed this as a sign directing me to my calling. I've been searching for my place in the cannabis world ever since. Even now, I continue to seek to establish myself in the culture. This book is a part of that journey. I'm proud that I'm finally able to finish it now.

***

Almost everyone in our business has experienced an arrest or robbery. Moreover, I have not met one person in the cannabis world who has been seriously physically or mentally hurt as a result of consuming cannabis. The reality is, many of the laws pertaining to growing and selling cannabis are still very problematic. While some countries have taken a more progressive approach toward marijuana, many places still have very harsh laws. The more I have written and traveled, the more I have found this to be true.

Countries that are more accepting of cannabis are currently in a transitional phase. Rules and regulations are constantly changing, slowly making business more feasible for some, but more difficult for most. The cost of cannabis — after all the taxes, fees and what have you — has formed a huge divide between the legal market and the black market.

This means that many lifelong cannabis advocates have been removed from the plant that they fought for and from the business that provided for them and their families financially. It's a struggle. In many ways, the problems of the past have not been solved through legalization. Some have been made worse.

For several years, I wrote articles for Treating Yourself. It was self-described as an alternative medical journal, but in reality, it was about marijuana. Almost every article and advertisement was geared toward cannabis or the community that surrounds it. However, at that time, they still had to hide. Nowadays, there are so many legal factors to consider with regard to cannabis. From obvious things, like magazines, to less obvious products related to growing. Then there are medical laws to consider in some states, and recreational laws in others. Of course, there are also CBD products in virtually every gas station and market across the country; there are all kinds of clothing and hemp-related products; there's glass paraphernalia and artwork. There are so many things to consider across so many different aspects of the industry. Some countries have gone further than the United States with regard to legalization, with no signs of any problems arising from these policy changes. Even with all the positive numbers legally and the slowly changing penalties, people are still getting arrested! In the streets, crime surrounding marijuana is still a rampant problem.

There are huge grey areas in new laws pertaining to cannabis, specifically when it comes to the differentiation between recreational and medical marijuana. State to state, these issues can be vastly different. As such, those who enter the business of selling cannabis and cannabis-related products are left scratching their heads and jumping through hoops to try to keep on top of the ever-changing laws. There are only a few states that have developed what purports to be an entirely legitimate system for people who want to grow marijuana and provide it to recreational users or medical patients, be it at a profit or not. This basically forces many marijuana growers to operate as if it were still entirely illegal. This includes those who are in the process of trying to make their businesses legal.

The majority of banks won't work with cannabis-related companies, so this makes things quite difficult. Deals are still often made with cash, under the radar of the local authorities. Business is carried out in cars, workplaces, hotel rooms and homes, where anything and everything can (and does) happen. Everyone in the business has heard of someone they know being robbed, arrested or worse. It's a dangerous game, despite the way it's portrayed in the entertainment industry. Popular culture representations couldn't be further from the truth as they omit the reality of the risks and consequences people face to make business possible. The positive side of things is thrust into the spotlight, and the negative side is usually so exaggerated that becomes fantastical or even comedic.

When I'm interviewed about my time working in the cannabis industry, people always ask about the negative stuff. Anything from close calls to the true stories of tragedy that I know of or have lived through personally. People love that side of things. While I receive a lot of support for my other accomplishments, most people want to hear about the scary stuff. This book is a collection of those bad experiences. I hope you enjoy them, but I also hope that they help some of you. Some names and details have been omitted or changed to protect those involved.

CHAPTER 1
THE AVERAGE STONER-TURNED-DEALER

I n school, I was not popular. Life was mundane and repetitive. I was looking for an escape. I had taken D.A.R.E. (Drug Abuse Resistance Education) classes in grade school, and when I found myself dwelling on my dissatisfaction in life and my lack of social status, I thought about what I had learned in D.A.R.E. It might sound kind of silly, but I thought about the way that the police officers had described drug users having or searching for an escape from reality. They were unhappy, and so, they used drugs to help them feel better. I thought about the euphoria that drugs supposedly provided these people, and although I knew it would be short-lived and possibly life-ruining, I started looking for my escape with drugs.

The first thing I found was my mom's cigarettes, which did make me feel better about myself, as I was doing something forbidden. However, it didn't provide me with the feelings I was looking for or the type of escape I craved

Next was alcohol. This was a much more difficult learning experience. I remember thinking that the stuff I was drinking must have gone bad, or that something had to be wrong with it. The harshness of my ingestion meant I didn't enjoy it; in fact, it felt like drinking fire. I wasn't drinking enough to get drunk or escape from my problems. The one time I did drink enough, I took it too far. I was so sick that I decided I never wanted to do it again.

Then I found marijuana. At first, it didn't really affect me much. Maybe I didn't take enough, but it had promise.

Marijuana was easy to consume. The smoke was more enjoyable than my mom's cigarettes, and it was a fast-acting substance. After a few minutes, I could gauge the degree to which it was affecting me and if I wanted more.

Dr. Dre's album "The Chronic" led to a huge increase in cannabis use. However, prior to this, Cypress Hill released a self-titled album that included multiple songs proclaiming their love of getting high. This was the first time I had ever heard someone depict smoking weed as cool and fun to do. Dr. Dre is often cited as a key influence, but I think the guys from Cypress Hill really deserve the credit for bringing cannabis into the mainstream for the kids of my generation.

Anyway, back to my story.

The first time I really got high was before watching the movie "Friday." My friends and I had all gathered at the United Artists Theater in North Hollywood to watch Ice Cube's character smoke weed. We had planned to get high, too, in solidarity, so that we could enjoy the movie in the correct state of mind. We walked across the street to the park, found a tree behind the tennis courts and started blazing it up.

Our friend had given us a broken ceramic pipe with a skull head bowl, and we could barely get the bowl loaded without blowing out the screen. We were total amateurs, but we managed to get a little high and walked over to the theater and enjoyed the movie. The feeling you get the first time you're high on cannabis differs from person to person, but for all of us, it was oddly similar.

All of us remember the experience vividly. We all felt light in the toes, almost as if we were walking on clouds. There was a feeling of disconnect, as if we were watching ourselves, rather than living our experiences. A clear haze seemed to fog my vision, and everything seemed much less serious and more enjoyable. Food tasted incredible. My thoughts were generally more pleasing. There was a very slight hint of exhaustion as I approached the end of my high. This was followed by a somewhat dirty feeling, as though I needed to eat a healthy meal to clean out my body. Aside from these aftereffects, the high was essentially harmless. I was in love, and, from that point on, when I could afford to get it, I would find it and enjoy.

My friends were not as into smoking pot as I was, but they would, on occasion, decide to get some or join me for a smoke.

Life moved on. Eventually, I got a job carpooling with an older Black gentleman who also smoked. He was far more experienced than me, and after a short amount of time working together, we were getting high every day before and after work. Eventually, we started getting high at lunch too.

It was getting expensive, even with my job, and so, I started buying in bulk to save more money. That is how it all began for me. Soon enough, I was selling off some of what I bought to pay for my own smoking habit.

I remember the first time I bought in bulk: an ounce for about $400. By the time I went out that night, I already had $400 back in my pocket. It was a really eye-opening experience, especially as someone who had never made more than minimum wage. Keep in mind that, at that time, everything was completely illegal, and there was no such thing as medical marijuana. For the next three years, I dealt out of my apartment — and had some very wild experiences.

Many of my stories from around that time are good fun, and the people involved were great friends. Hell, this was possibly the best time of my life. But I had no idea then how risky it really was.

CHAPTER 2
BREAKING MY DOOR DOWN

y first robbery was about a year or so into living in Encino, California. I had a third-floor apartment facing the freeway, so it wasn't very well hidden. When I first moved in, I thought I could maybe grow enough marijuana for myself so that I wouldn't need to buy any.

This was a short-lived plan, but after a good friend suffered some unfortunate circumstances with the police, I offered to help him out. I began keeping his pot at my place because he was unsure if it would be safe to keep at home. This led to me selling to my friends.

The first couple of times it happened, it was like a magic trick. I would buy an ounce, split it up, sell it and end up with all the money I had paid plus a bunch of leftover pot I could smoke myself. It was great. Gradually, people started to come to me more and more until I was basically a regular pot dealer.

People I knew would send their friends by sometimes, and I would take care of their orders. I had around 30 or 40 people who would periodically come by to hang out and smoke. There were a few people I had gone to school with and had known for a while, so they were around my place often and could have seen where I kept things hidden.

One friend, from Hungary, was the roommate of the guy who had helped me out when I was getting started selling pot. This particular friend of mine was hard to get along with. He didn't have a lot of friends, so he spent a good bit of time hanging out at my place. He was a former heroin user and kept a bad crowd, but he was a good guy when he was sober. Some of his friends made their own pills and robbed people, and he eventually fell back into doing heroin. I really struggled with this. He was my friend, but he was very confrontational. When he would bring his drugs to my apartment and use them there, I just didn't know what to do or what to say to him.

He eventually started smoking heroin in front of me. I had no idea how to stop it without causing more problems. So I tried to avoid him when I could, and I vented to our other friends. This was not the right thing to do. He ultimately got pissed off with me and argued that I thought I was better than him.

He came over less and less, and I heard that he had encountered serious problems. He was selling less pot and had moved on to drugs with harsher penalties, like ecstasy. Eventually, he was robbed. I think he even got arrested too. He lost his place and ended up living in his car around the corner from my apartment. Almost all his friends had turned their backs on him by this point.

I came home after work one day, and my door had been kicked in. The deadbolt was bent, and the locks were smashed. The wood frame was broken, and there were splinters everywhere. The door handle was completely warped, and the locks were so twisted and bent out of shape that I couldn't believe someone had managed to cause such damage in the middle of the day in such an open public area of our complex. It must have been loud, yet none of my neighbors had heard anything.

My house was torn apart. Specific areas had clearly been rummaged through, while other areas remained in perfect condition. My glass pipes and bongs had all been stolen, except for one special one named "Skeletor" that was hidden in plain view and had somehow avoided the rampage.

My money was gone, and my marijuana was gone. Believe it or not, I actually called the police. I didn't tell them all the details, just that I had been robbed. They sent someone out to check on it and, a couple days later, sent another person to do fingerprinting. The police made no effort to find the perpetrator. My former friend eventually admitted to another friend that he had done it, but I never saw him again. He ran into more problems through other criminal activities, and the last I heard, he had been deported back to Hungary.

CHAPTER 3
LATE NIGHT HOME INVASION

My second robbery was a bad one — possibly my worst. I had reconnected with some girls that I used to know back in high school. They came over to buy pot from me fairly often. It was fun, and they would share crazy stories about their wild lives. They had a lot of friends that I had hung out with when I was younger, and they would tell me about how their lives had changed and the new drugs and other experiences they were into. The girls told me that they were bisexual and that sometimes they would hook up with each other. I found one of them in particular very attractive, so that was cool.

They always had a lot of drama to discuss, and I would often give them advice and try to help them out if I could. We were close. Sometimes, we would disagree, but usually, we all got along great. Eventually, they started bringing old friends of mine back around again, and one of them ended up bringing over someone who was into heroin. It wasn't the former friend who robbed me, but they were the same kind of person. This eventually led to more trouble.

The attractive girl started stripping at a place nearby and would often ask me to come visit her. I never did, so she decided she would work off some of her debt to me by coming over and cleaning my condo. I actually really needed this service, so I accepted her offer, and we arranged a time for her to come round and clean.

She arrived, went upstairs to my bedroom and got undressed. I came up to show her what to do and there she was ... naked. I told her she needed to get dressed and start cleaning. She could tell I was serious, and she then started cleaning my condo as we had agreed. I didn't sleep with her, and I think she was offended by this because she came over much less frequently after that. I also noticed she was being very crafty with her work at the strip club and the people she was seeing there. Soon after I noticed this, I got a visit.

I was at home, seeing people as I normally would. I always had loads of people over. We would talk for hours, and I hooked them all up. We would all smoke and have a great time together. It was fun, and sometimes, we even did a little extra partying with some cocaine I would pick up from a friend.

I had recently scored some really good weed. Some of it had been dished out to other people, but I still had most of it left over. For the longest time, I kept all my valuable stuff in a safe, but one stoned night, I decided it was probably a bad idea to keep things in there, and came up with a secret hiding place. That day, once everyone had left, I passed out in a corner of my living room. I woke to find a person standing over me.

It was not someone I knew. After I realized what was going on, I sat up quickly. Two other guys were going around my place and taking things. They saw I was now awake and came over to me. One cocked his gun at me. He told me they were not playing around, and they demanded I give them all my weed and money. I immediately looked over to my table where I kept a small amount out to serve to people. They had already cleared it out. I thought about all the weed that I had hidden in my freezer inside food boxes. I made sure to not look toward the kitchen and told them they had everything.

When they found my safe, and I couldn't open it, they messed with me for a while. They had taken my keys, and I couldn't find them. They punched me in the face and told me that they were going to tie me up.

I had seen all their faces, so I was a little worried when they said that. I thought about every movie I had seen where they kill the witnesses. I willingly sat down and let them start to tie me up. They didn't have zip ties or anything like that. Instead, they had some kind of string or rope that was difficult to work with, and they were having trouble. While tying me up, one of them became more violent, demanding I tell him where everything was. When I told him nothing, he said they were going to kill me.

My first thought was, "I am not going out like this." I jumped from my seat and broke free of my poorly wrapped ties. They grabbed me immediately and held the gun to my face. They made me lie on the floor. They argued amongst themselves, yelling at the guy who had said they would kill me. They told him to shut up and that it wasn't their plan to do that.

One had grabbed a suitcase of mine and filled it with all kinds of valuables: my DVDs, a friend's Nintendo 64 that I had borrowed. Anything fun or of value, they took. They even took some of my shoes.

One of them told me that they knew I had more marijuana, and that they even knew exactly how much I had, so I should just give it up. That was a scary moment, and I had to think quickly. I told them I had fronted all the weed to a few people who had been there earlier that night. Fronting was common, and it basically meant I gave the pot to someone else without getting paid, kind of like consignment, with the promise that they would pay me back later when it was sold. This took them off the trail completely.

Eventually, they decided to take my safe with them. They took my car keys and my house keys. While they hadn't smashed my door or my locks, I was still just as terrified as I would have been if the door had been wide open.

They made me lie down on the floor and count to 100. So that's what I did. I was still afraid to get up even when it was over.

Eventually, I did get up. I went downstairs and called a friend who lived up off Balboa. He was a great guy, and he came over to help me out. I didn't call the cops this time because they had been useless the first time. I told my parents I was robbed, though, and they tried to help me out with some of my bills. I was overwhelmingly glad that the robbers hadn't found my secret hiding place. Otherwise, they would have taken my entire inventory.

I sold off what I still had, and I was back in the swing of things right away. I was, however, very traumatized from the experience.

I don't think I have ever been the same since. The memory haunted me, and I worried about it for years, scared they would come back or that I'd see them at a party. The expense of getting new keys for my car and for my place was a drag, but I got it all sorted.

From what I heard from her friends later, the robbers were most likely friends of the girl I wouldn't sleep with. It was never 100% confirmed, but I was fairly sure it was her idea.

Oh, and they missed Skeletor again.

CHAPTER 4
MEETING AT THE IRON DOOR

You'd think I would have learned my lesson after getting robbed twice, but I was young, and I had not.

After I had successfully avoided her for a while, the girl that had been potentially responsible for my home invasion began to hit me up for weed from time to time. I was stupid and desperate for money, so I would sell it to her. Although I still suspected that she was the one who had set me up, I wasn't 100% sure, so I gave her the benefit of the doubt. She and her girlfriend would come over sometimes. It wasn't as it had been before, but they came round often enough for me to become familiar with them again.

Around this time, the brother of the other girl — the not-so-hot one — was also coming over frequently with his girlfriend. They would pick up pot, and they'd hang out and talk with me for a while. We were mostly cool, but I can sometimes be condescending, and I was probably a little mean to him on a few occasions.

I tried to be as fair as possible, but every now and then, I would have to stop fronting weed because people wouldn't pay. Unfortunately, he was one of those people. I would only help him when he could pay, and he was a tad bitter about it.

I should have been smarter, but at that time, I trusted people too easily. We had been casually talking about all the things I had done to level up the security at my place — and I had unwittingly told him everything he'd need to know to get inside. I told him that I was worried because, even though I had a steel door, there was probably a tool that could slice it like butter. He must have gone and done his research.

I came home a bit late one evening. I was meeting a girl I was dating back at my place. She was also running late, and coincidently, we both arrived at the same time.

My front door was torn to pieces. The metal mesh had been pulled back and split open, with sharp shards still left sticking out. The wooden door had been kicked in. This time, they had found all of my pipes and bongs, even the ones hidden in places only a friend would know. They even took Skeletor. There was not much else for them to steal, as I only had a small amount of weed. There was about an ounce or so, but they took it nonetheless.

The only saving grace was that I had just paid for me and my friends to go to Amsterdam. I had had about $10,000 the day before, but I had just paid the travel company, so all that was left was a few hundred bucks. I had also bought a really cool pipe to take with me to Amsterdam, but that had been taken. I was devastated. I called the police, and once again, they did nothing.

That weekend, I moved all my stuff into my parents' garage. I broke ties with everyone I didn't know well. I sold my place for double what I had bought it for, and I came out way ahead of the game.

It was a strange transition, but I think it was the best road for me to go down. I've never been able to build my life back up to what it was. I've never experienced that degree of popularity or that much fun, but I have felt safer and calmer. For me, that's the better position to be in. I never did hear from the girl's brother again, but I've always assumed it was him. His sister always spoke carefully around me afterward, so this somewhat confirmed my suspicions. It was probably him, but I guess I will never know for sure.

All my friends were wonderful. They came to my aid when I needed them, helping me move all my stuff. We boxed everything up, and it was all done so quickly. Another friend charged me a reasonable amount to fix up the condo. I struggled to pay, after everything that had happened, but I made it work, and it really paid off.

Once I sold the place, I was able to pay off my car loan. I even had enough left to make a down payment on another place. This time, I moved to a safer neighborhood, in Hollywood. This was a good decision, but my business suffered, and I really had to tighten the belt for a long time. It was definitely safer, but the need for money meant that I took more risks. This eventually led me down a bad path.

CHAPTER 5
A SHORT PERIOD OF LUCK AND TRANSFORMATION

A significant amount of time passed before I ran into trouble again. A lot had happened over the years, and the culture of marijuana was changing in California. The introduction of medical marijuana dispensaries was the biggest change. With this, so many things came to pass. Before the medical scene, however, there was the Kush phenomenon.

Kush was basically a genotype: a specific genetic strain of marijuana. It was gaining popularity because it was incredibly potent. It had a distinct smell and taste, and even a discernible texture. There are many stories as to how it came about. It became hugely popular, and it changed the way marijuana was grown and sold in Southern California.

People would pay more money for this type of weed, and so, it became an issue of supply and demand. Some buyers would only buy this kind of marijuana, so people started to try and grow more. Then others started to try and grow different versions of it. The price skyrocketed, and people would pay double for the best quality. Dealers typically carried some kind of Kush along with their regular Chronic. There were also other lower grades of marijuana, called Stress or Mexican; sometimes, it was just called Cents.

Shortly after Kush became the rage, the medical marijuana dispensaries started to open. They were small at first, and they didn't have access to the best Kush, but they did have connections to growers who were developing unique strains that many people were not familiar with, such as Blue Dot and Purple Urkle. These strains were strong and unique in their own ways. The increased access to new flavors brought about an increase in available hash. Of course, Kush eventually made its way into the shops as well. During this time, there were a few years where the best weed and hash available came from the dispensaries.

At this point, I was a home dealer trying to find my own way in the world. When Kush first emerged, I avoided selling it. I mostly just tried to max out my deals on other quality pot. Eventually, I was sold some top-quality Kush. I started selling it for $90 an eighth and $30 a gram. It was very good pot, and to this day, I have trouble finding stuff as good as this was. My clientele had dwindled when I moved, but this was enough to bring them back. My prices were a bit higher, so I was not attracting the lower-class crowd that I had dealt with in the past. This was a blessing in disguise.

I was doing alright selling Kush and the regular Chronic from my house, but I had been told about the dispensaries and decided to give them a try and see what they had. I was actually a perfect fit as a medical patient because I was genuinely sick, and I used marijuana to alleviate my symptoms. I had problems with abdominal pain, and I was allergic to various foods. I now know much more about how diet-related my problems were. Pot helped me eat and feel less nauseous. I went online to look up how to get my medical marijuana identification card, and then I went out and got one. It was rather easy to do, and the whole experience was quite strange. This would allow me to go to dispensaries and legally possess a certain amount of marijuana for my personal use.

After receiving my letter of recommendation, I found two local marijuana dispensaries that were really close to my place. My first visit was both awesome and terrifying. I was overjoyed to see marijuana being treated in the States like it was treated in Amsterdam, and I was pleased that it was available in so many flavors. However, from a business perspective, I was horrified to see something I could not compete with. I worried that I wouldn't be able to make money selling pot the way I had been doing. I had a love-hate relationship with the shops for a while, but I eventually found a way to start working with them.

At first, I simply bought from them and resold the weed at a slightly higher price. I found a good margin to buy at a bulk price, and I was able to distribute it at a little less of a profit than I had been making before. That worked out, and eventually, the Kush prices started to come down because people were going to the dispensaries more and more often. It was really interesting to see happen. I had to have the expensive Kush, then the slightly less expensive medical pot, and then the regular Chronic or the Regs. Slowly but surely, my home business dropped off to damn near nothing, and I had to find a way to make more money.

The entire time I was dealing, I also maintained a regular day job. I began by working various jobs in the telecommunications field. Later, I worked at Magic Mountain, then The Broadway department store. Then I ended up working with my dad, and that's where I stayed for a long time. At some point, that job started to become a problem for me because of the family interaction and the work itself dried up, I also wasn't the best at it. Thankfully, I had a friend who wanted to invest with me, and we decided to start a grow operation together.

I rented the place, and another one of my friends entered as a partner and wanted to handle the buildout. This was a big mistake on my part, but I let him do it, and he spent all our money. It was a very elaborate setup, but it was worth about a third of what he actually spent putting it together. We had a falling out, and he left me on my own to make this grow happen. I tried to bring in different people, but it just never worked.

The main problem was that the guy who set everything up was a grower. I had chosen him to be part of the project because I had known him for a while, and he was good at what he did. I had watched his grow go from poor to extremely profitable in just a few years. He had learned what he needed to know, and he had worked with people who helped him get to where he needed to be. I thought working with him would give me a head start, as he had already overcome all of these problems.

He was, however, insanely lazy. I had heard about the problems he had encountered in the past, but I never thought that he might have been the root of his own issues. I talked with him about the project, and he entered into the agreement with the right attitude. After a short amount of time, he decided he was not up to it and that I was not doing my fair share of the work. This was probably about three weeks into our very first harvest. He decided he would let me continue on my own, and that's when I took over and started trying to find someone else to fill in. He had built the place with his own specific techniques in mind, and so, I had trouble finding someone else who worked the way he did.

Grower after grower told me how much he had spent and how I had been taken advantage of. All kinds of equipment had been implemented and installed incorrectly. So much money had been wasted. It was staggering, and I found myself grasping at straws to find someone to help. I managed to find a friend who needed to move into a new place, and he told me he could help. Unfortunately, he did the bare minimum, and I damn near lost the entire harvest. From the 30 pounds, we got 9. Once again, I had to try to find someone else.

This time, I let my partner have at it, and they found someone who also told us everything we wanted to hear. When the time came, he couldn't produce either. By this point, we had worked with him for a long time. We had brought him to shows and really introduced him into the scene. I couldn't get him to where we needed him to be, and I ended up losing all my own money, as well as the funds from my investors. It was a terrible situation, and every month, we were struggling. Looking back on it, I probably should have just done it all myself, but my experiences with much smaller growing situations were poor to average at best.

My new partner's harvests weren't particularly good quality either. The results ranged from average to terrible. I had to drop prices and try anything I could to find people to buy our marijuana. I found places that would try it for a while, but eventually they didn't want it anymore. I was constantly trying to find new ways to make a few hundred bucks. It was not a good situation to be in, and slowly, I found myself doing increasingly risky things to try to get ahead. This led me to my next bad experience and the Hemp Con.

CHAPTER 6
SURPRISE INVASION

decided to go back to trying to maximize my smaller sales. I started trying out new people in order to make up for the much-needed increase in sales to get enough money to pay my bills. This went well at first, because my profit on moving larger weight was low and my own grow was not staggered, so I was getting enough of a yield to make selling my pounds at a low cost an option. Granted I was still selling them slowly at smaller amounts, but the total value was higher, so it made it all worth it. I could sell a pound in ounces and make much more than if I sold it all at once. There were various people I met doing this and they were all great for the most part. Like anything though, one bad apple can ruin the bunch.

I had a few friends that I had met through some other friends that did bar tending work for Wolfgang Puck. These new friends were basically poor people who were just scraping by in society, not really that much different from myself. There was a girl who was nice but often misguided and then there was a guy who always came with her, I thought they were together, but she always said things kind of flirting with me, making me think they were not. He was into heavy metal but didn't have much else going on and looked really out of shape & bad off. The girl was really nice and even attractive but also not well off. They always paid for their weed though and seemed like they were decent people just trying to make it by. Eventually the girl brought over her brother, who was a super scary guy like a character from a movie, but he really liked me and became a fairly good customer for a while. They came over off and on for a few years, and there was never a problem with them directly.

One time the guy brought a black guy he met at the weed shop by who he said was his friend. This guy bought an ounce a couple times and was cool enough. Another time he called me to get an ounce, and I didn't respond right away, so he got kinda pissed and I could tell something was up with him but I couldn't tell if he was just having a bad day or what. He arranged to come over and so I met him at my place. I also had a friend with me at home doing some trimming from my last grow harvest. Before the guy showed up he called, and I ran around the house loosely hiding things because of my prior bad experiences and it just isn't a good idea to let people see you have pounds sitting around the house. Temptation can be a real nasty thing, especially mixed with assuming someone is well off. I also put a bit more pot in my table jar that I used to weigh out people's orders. I kept a smaller amount visible for sales that had worked well as a distraction in the past. Then he buzzed at the front door.

I let him in and he went and stood by my friend at the couch, then just as I was closing the door another big guy came around the corner, so I let him in too. This is often a thing that happens, and people bring their friends to meet me, sometimes it would lead to new business. There was a weird vibe coming off them both as they asked for an ounce. I started to weigh it out and I was basically waiting for them to do something. As the big guy tried to pull out his gun, I saw it and I grabbed it and tried to take it from him. He got all flustered, I almost got it, but he wrestled it away from me then told me I was crazy and to go sit on the couch. My friend was begging them to take everything and to just leave as soon as possible but he was very levelheaded about it. I was going nuts and telling them this can't be happening, and I was not gonna let this happen. I was freaking out, and I was getting up and sitting down, moving all around. This made them angry and the one guy who had been over before started to get crazy with me, he busted out zip ties and called someone else on the phone, told them my unit number and said to come inside.

I was now totally freaked out and I jumped up and started to yell for help. The first guy attacked me, he punched my face and slammed me down on my couch. The big guy with the gun just told his buddy that he was going to shoot me and get it over with. Then my friend got up and started to help them get my stuff together and get out as fast as possible, and I was fine with that at the time. He cleared off my table and there was a bunch of miscommunication between the two robbers. Was this going to be enough for them or not, they were arguing. As soon as he let me go I was up and approaching the big one with the gun telling them to just get out. I quickly slipped by him and opened my front door. They started to go but were slow and hesitating, so I pushed the big 300+ pound one right out my front door. The other guy grabbed me from behind and slammed me to the floor. I immediately stood up and they both looked at each other and took off running.

I shut the door and locked it and thanked my friend for his help. We were both totally flustered for a long while, but he had helped me save what was probably about 10 pounds of marijuana variously stashed around my house, worth say $40,000 or so and for the retail value say just about double that. The robbers did get something, basically 2 ounces and about 20 grams of some hash, or roughly anywhere from $1000 to as much as maybe $2000 worth of cannabis. Plus a bunch of various other things like some shake, a bunch of trim and stems etc. It was a really odd thing that I would end up so lucky in so many ways, while still being so unlucky as to have this happen to me yet again.

I immediately tried to call the heavy metal latino guy who introduced me to this other guy. No answer, and so I also called the girls brother who loved me but was a complete criminal. Later that day I got a call back from the Latino guy and he was saying he didn't know anything about it. I could tell something was up with him and so I cut him off. The next day the girls brother came to see me, he told me the Latino guy was involved and was asking where I kept my larger amounts. Seemed like they were going to maybe come back so he left me one of his guns and instructed me exactly how to use it because it was very small. I kept it for a while, they never came back and I stopped talking to the Latino guy and the girl. I eventually gave the gun back and shortly after that guy went to prison for some crime again. I'm almost positive he killed people before and who knows what else he had done. This was it for me and selling pot out of my house and so I began to try and find another way to make money.

CHAPTER 7
A HEMP CON

n Los Angeles, there were a few cannabis-related trade shows that took place at the Convention Center and various other locations around the city. These kinds of shows, geared toward the cannabis-related product industry, were completely legal. There were nutrient lines, glass pipe companies — everything you can imagine that might be related to marijuana. I would work some of the shows for companies I was connected to, or sometimes, I would attend them for fun or to see friends. Occasionally, I would bring things to sell.

At one show, I ran into a couple of people I had come to know from a company that was making a football-related marijuana smoking game. It was the only game related to marijuana at the time, and it was run by some very good but troubled folks. Each of them had their issues, like most people do. They were pumping out products and promoting this game, and their crew attended all the events. We got to talking with some of the guys from one of the teams, and they said they were looking for weight. They gave me some huge numbers, but I only had a couple of pounds with me in my car. I shouldn't have mentioned this, but I thought they were friends and part of the game company's team.

They told me that they could flip it quickly around the corner from the event. They made a few calls and came back to find me, telling me it was on. We would have to show the guy the stuff before he bought it, which was pretty normal. I went down with them to my car, and as we were walking, I started having second thoughts. One guy was talking my ear off, really overselling how much he had helped people I know. I thought it sounded like it might be a rip-off, but I gave them the benefit of the doubt.

I unlocked my car and gave them the box I had with the 2 pounds in it. Walking to their car, things started getting strange. The guy I was most familiar with went over and started talking to someone else, while the new guy I had met that day put the box in his car. I started to get into their car, but the new guy was driving and told me that I couldn't go with them to sell it. He called his buddy to come back. I thought maybe they didn't want me to know how much they were going to make. As he was getting into the car, I made him give me his number and tell me what the plan was. They assured me everything was going to be all good and that I should wait for them by the stage. I waited all night.

I was stressing out throughout the entirety of the show. I approached his friends, and they all told me he was not to be trusted. Some went out of their way to try and help me, but they didn't get the weed back. They just stopped talking to him. I tried over and over again with one friend of theirs. He said he was going to get the weed back, then he was going to give me some other weed, then just their address, but he always flaked out. The guys who stole the cannabis at the trade show would even try to contact me to make it right. They did so a bunch of times, but all in all, it just led to more smoke screens, and it didn't solve the problem. Their friend finally gave me the addresses of the people who stole the cannabis, and I passed that along to someone who said they were going to take care of it. To my knowledge, they never did.

CHAPTER 8
GETTING ARRESTED

After all those troubles, I was able to strike up a business deal with a friend from the trade shows. He lived out of state and wanted to bring in cannabis from California to sell at a profit. I got some offers for pounds we could sell, but he had a guy he wanted me to work with, so I met him and started doing drives across the state.

The plan worked seamlessly. I developed a customer base with the original product, and then, I would source some higher quality cannabis from other people to see if that would sell. We made thousands of dollars each trip, and it was quickly becoming my most profitable venture thus far. We would get the orders lined up between the two of us, and then, it was just a matter of arranging everything in each state. I would drive to the distributor, who would then supply me with, say, 20 pounds, give or take, and then, we would seal it all up properly. Most times, I'd do the drive directly from there, but other times, I would have to stop off and go the next day. There was an office space the distributor had rented. He had a trailer there that was all locked up and sealed for smell. I would pull my car in, and we would shut the gate and get to work. As soon as we were done, I drove right out and went on my way.

Typically, we got pre-orders together and then arranged a time with the distributor for pickup. From there, I would head out across state lines and get to my location a few hours later. I would stay for several days with my friend, and each day, we would meet up with various people, move the grass and get the money. I would bring it all in suitcases in a rental car. There wasn't much planning to it. I started to notice people randomly getting pulled over in the city, so I mentioned to my friend that we needed a plan if I were to ever get pulled over. He thought I was being paranoid, telling me numerous times how he smoked in his car doing the drive I was doing, and so, we never came up with a good script in case I got pulled over. This, of course, would eventually become a problem.

It was a great way of making money for a while, and we did it regularly every month or two. Something worthwhile would come around, and we would split the profits. I was enjoying the change in lifestyle, so we added a few people to the orders.

We had a close call on one occasion. I went with a friend to meet a new guy who was putting in orders. He had an apartment in a large complex. We met in the parking lot and were doing business in his SUV. Finishing up, we exchanged the money and the product. As I was getting out of the car to get back into my own, I noticed a police car slowly drive into the parking lot. The policemen were looking around as if they were trying to find something out of place. I turned to him as I got out and popped my head back in his front window to let him know what was happening.

We didn't set off any red flags, so the police car slowly drove past us and turned. We moved quickly. I got into my car and started to drive away. I noticed the cruiser reversing, and I thought the police were going to drive back up the way they came. I wondered if they were following me, or if they had gone back to talk to my friends, who were still in their car in the parking lot. I drove the rental car around the corner out of sight and quickly made my way to the back of a lot. I parked and hid so that I could see what was going on. I didn't see any of the cars drive out, so after about 15 minutes, I decided to drive away. From what I heard, nothing happened. I'm not sure what would have happened if they had approached us, but fortunately, I made it home without a problem.

My next visit did not go well. I brought another bunch of cannabis. This time it was probably close to 30 pounds. We sold most of it over the course of three or four days. We met some football players and some other folks, but nobody who seemed like they might be an obvious problem. We decided I should go home and leave what I hadn't sold because my friend in Arizona could probably get rid of it over the next few days.

I prepared myself to head back across the border. I was seeing a girl at the time too. She had various mental problems, and she wanted me to come back into town. In a hurry to get back, I headed out a bit earlier than I normally would have liked to. On the way back, I stopped to eat somewhere, and that was that. No red flags.

Nothing seemed out of the ordinary to me while driving, and I made decent time. There is a point before the border to California where there is a long stretch of a two-lane highway. Often, a cop car parks in the center divider watching traffic, probably looking for speeders. I was driving along when I saw a car like this parked a few miles ahead. I took my foot off the accelerator for a moment and checked my speed. I then proceeded as if nothing were amiss. As I passed the car, it started to leave the center divider, but it had to wait for a clear spot. I got about 3 miles ahead, and then, I decided to pull into the slow lane and wait for them to drive by. The cop car approached me and drove next to my car, keeping pace with me for a few hundred feet or so. It was really strange, like they were specifically looking for me.

They pulled in behind me in the slow lane, put on their lights and pulled me over. I was ready. I made my way to the side of the road and stopped. I had no idea what I had done to warrant them pulling me over, though I assumed the worst. No laws had been broken at any point from the moment I saw them to when I was pulled over, and this made me very suspicious.

The officer approached my window and asked for my driver's license. I immediately asked why he had pulled me over, and he said the strangest thing: "I'm pulling you over for going too slow and not letting the faster cars drive by." This made no sense. I had been in the slow lane in front of a semitruck when the cop had pulled me over. I had been there for a few minutes when they caught back up with me. I might have had a chance if I had confronted him immediately about this accusation. He said something about the smell of marijuana and asked me to get out of the car, but he also assured me that nothing was wrong.

As I walked around to talk to the officer, he asked a very young girl in regular clothing to come over to observe or something. I had not seen her until she got out of the cruiser, and when I saw her, I thought I was being set up. I was certain that I had never seen this girl before.

The officer began to question me, and I tried to answer as best I could. However, when I realized it was not going well, I stopped talking and told him I would need to speak to an attorney. He arrested me as soon as I said that. They searched my car and found my backpack, where I had a legal amount of cannabis and about $30,000 in cash. They also found the empty suitcase. I was in the back of his car for a while. We drove for what seemed like an eternity, and eventually, I was taken in to talk to detectives. I was questioned and threatened, but ultimately, they let me talk to a famous cannabis attorney and he told me what to do. They got in touch with my family, who bailed me out of prison the next day. I spent the rest of the week in town, staying at a friend's place and trying to find an attorney educated on cannabis to defend me, which eventually I did. Coincidentally, it was Lil Wayne's attorney. I had to tell the others involved about the situation. Everyone was concerned and helpful.

The cops were not done yet. Eventually, they set up my friend and came to arrest him. He was growing in his house and still moving product despite knowing everything that had happened to me. He was one plant over the limit, and they got him on that. We both had a long ordeal, and somehow, he ended up with worse penalties. My attorney thought they must have been watching him for a variety of reasons, but it made me straighten up. When I was going to court, the attorney's assistant told me some horrifying things the police had said. One was about my phone. At this time, I was writing for Treating Yourself magazine. There were lots of pictures of weed farms and other related stuff they thought were a gold mine. By the time my case was heard, the prosecution apparently had a stack of documents about me that was almost a foot tall.

My attorney told me that everything was already arranged with the prosecution and that it would be quick. But when he finally came out to see me, he was visibly shaken, very nervous — and I'm not sure it was helpful for me to talk to him at that point. He told me that the police had a mountain of information about me, and they had been discussing how they could get me for four hours, what the results of their efforts would be, and if it was worth it to move forward with any of the charges they were contemplating.

The attorney said he had never experienced anything like this. I had hired this attorney because he had defended big criminals and had told me about some other heinous situations he had worked through. He was reassuring me as much as he could, but he was also playing damage control, saying he was still expecting the same result we had discussed, but that, after seeing how they were going after me, anything was possible. He said that I could end up dealing with some charges. He went back into the meeting, and I was told to wait for him to call me. I got off with a slap on the wrist, but it cost me a lot of money, and I still haven't financially recovered from that day. My next adventures in the world of cannabis would need to be in a somewhat legal or defensible area. Luckily, I found that place rather quickly.

CHAPTER 9
WHEN THE POLICE SHOWED UP IN RIOT GEAR

Time went by, and after a while, I began to form the Secret Cup: a cannabis concentrate competition and award ceremony in Los Angeles. The first event was organized by my friend Big D in Denver, Colorado, and was merged with NikkaT's event, Extract Artists Unite. Cannabis events were not a new thing, but there were only a couple that could be considered successful. Some were huge celebrations and competitions, but most were just small parties. A few were fashion shows and food-related events, but most served as settings for people to sell cannabis-related stuff (and actual cannabis under the table). I had been going to these events for years. While I enjoyed them a great deal, it was obvious they were not as popular as other mainstream events, and for a long while, many of the best cannabis-related events were not even in the United States.

The most well-known competition had become somewhat discredited by rumors of fraud and corruption. Most of these accusations were likely false, but I also knew people who had confessed to taking part in what could only be described as an agreement wherein they purchased their awards by making "donations" or paying for large sponsorship contracts. More stories were being told, but I hadn't personally seen any real evidence. I had assumed that most of the winners that hadn't made sense to me had won authentic victories because of poor judging. However, the public had, for the most part, made up their mind based on the simple rumor of fraud. It was a big problem. Everyone in the community at the time knew about it, and nobody was happy about it.

That's how the Secret Cup came to be.

Big D had competed in various events and had won first prize at a few, but he wasn't often the top-prize winner. In some competitions, the results didn't seem to represent the authentic best entries. The high cost of entry fees also kept some of the people with the absolute highest-quality products from being able to compete. The competitions were either too expensive to enter, or the amount of product required wasn't feasible. In some cases, they demanded more quantity than could even be made, let alone given away for free for a no-cash prize. The only prize, other than the physical trophies that were awarded, was word of mouth. The winners hoped that enough people would hear or read about their product and that this would generate more sales. However, this did not always happen, and the fraud rumors further revealed a need for something better.

After discussing these problems with some of his peers, Big D wanted to host a private competition that had vastly different rules. He wanted to ensure more people could meet the competition's entry requirements. The idea was that these changes would result in a more authentic winner. This became an entire movement. So many people wanted the same thing, and the hype around it grew fast. As I mentioned, Big D had joined forces with NikkaT's, who was gaining a big following at that time. NikkaT's cannabis experience was based around concentrates made without solvents, and because he was a former reggae DJ, he brought with him a party perspective. It made sense to merge the two events.

I initially started to write about it in Treating Yourself magazine, but I soon realized they needed more help. Because I had extensive experience in the hash world, I began helping right away. Honestly, I really had nothing better to do.

Colorado was scheduled to legalize cannabis recreationally just before the competition was scheduled to take place. The state then announced a potential delay, one that could make hosting the party less legal. We discussed this a great deal, and we decided to continue as planned. Just before the event, the state legalized cannabis in one of those closed-door secret overnight meetings, and so, we woke up to the glorious resolution of the problem. The event was a cannabis competition like no other, and it was wonderful to experience. The hype thereafter exploded organically. The show had been an inspirational success. I approached Big D and told him that, with his consent, I would be interested in doing the same thing in Los Angeles, despite the difference in laws.

The scene in Colorado was good, but the world of cannabis in California was legendary. As time passed, I realized that the only way to move forward was to start planning the event myself. We went over the details and established how the first competition had worked. I personally rewrote the rules, and I started looking to secure a venue. There were ups and downs to this process. I looked at a few places, and most were too small to host an event that would require vendor booths. I found a couple of promoters who got paid for finding venues for underground rave parties, and they began to help me. I decided that this was the most logical way for me to find a venue. I had had friends who were involved in this kind of thing growing up, and I had seen them make rave culture become what it is today. I was introduced to a guy who supposedly had a great location. I went to see it, and I knew it could work. At the time, I was fortunate enough to still have a little side income from my screen-printing company, Rig Rags, and some other black-market business I was still into, so I started making reservations.

Any somewhat-legitimate venue would inevitably find out about the cannabis aspect of the event and cancel out of fear of legal repercussions. This was a huge problem. One venue said we could have cannabis-related things but no smoking or sales of actual cannabis products. This became routine, and every place we went to look at took issue with the event.

Even places that had done various kinds of cannabis events before informed us that they had been legally instructed to never host another. After all this, it was no surprise that when the venue scout and I went to meet the owners of the venue we liked, he told me not discuss the cannabis elements of the event. This was fine by me at first, but as time went on, it became more and more clear to me that keeping this a secret could result in a much bigger problem closer to or even during the actual show. I made it clear to my venue scout that we needed to be honest, and he assured me that he had had a talk with them and that everything was fine. I paid him a fee and put money down to reserve the venue, but he was very careful about allowing me to go to the location without him.

Eventually, he introduced me to the "owner" of the building. I went to meet him at home. He seemed like he was on some kind of drug and came across as quite shady. I was suspicious. With the event date getting closer, I decided to go to the venue myself and see what I could dig up. With only 10 days to go, I discovered that the scout had not reserved the location or discussed the details with them at all. There was an office at the venue, and I spoke to the person in charge. She told me there was no possible way their attorney would have approved of the cannabis portion of the event. They did have room, but nothing was scheduled to take place. Sure enough, a couple of days later, the attorney called me to make it very clear that no event of this kind would be permitted. I desperately had to try to recover the money that I had put down with the venue scout and find a new venue that could handle all the booths, the VIP area, the stage and what have you, not to mention the glass blowing.

I looked at maybe 10 other warehouse party locations over the next few days. I finally found a new place. A friend of mine knew this guy in the trance electronic music scene. He showed me a spot called Swede Studios in downtown LA. It was like night and day compared to the other venue. It was in a bad neighborhood but big enough to handle everything, so it was a go. I was crafty and got the other venue scout to meet me at another potential venue location. I made it clear that I needed to get my money back, and he gave me what he was able to. It was nearly the entire amount, so I left it at that and never heard from him again. I arranged all the plans for the replacement venue, and it was looking great.

As the event date approached, many people who had thought we couldn't do it started trying to get involved. It was really interesting to see the different attitudes from the people in the industry. Some were very supportive and put their money in right away. Others acted like they didn't want to be involved, only to show up the day of the event and try to buy their way into being a part of it.

This was one of the first times I got to see how some of the "industry leaders" conducted themselves, and how their real personalities contrasted with their public personas. Some reluctantly supported the show but also mocked it at the same time, saying careless, hurtful things that could be damaging. Others showed what awesome people they were and rolled with the punches like real outlaws and veterans of the cannabis war. The event was chaotic from the get-go, and it was really popular. We packed the venue to its absolute maximum. At one point, the venue owners came to complain and told me they were "cool with weed smoking but didn't realize everyone who smoked weed in Los Angeles would be there." Our mark was made right away. This was the greatest revolution many of us had experienced in cannabis for a while, and people were ready for a change. There was a little more to the story, of course.

As I mentioned before, I had been seeing a girl who had some personal problems, and we had been having various issues as a result. I admit that some of them were my fault. She had a boyfriend of sorts, and I probably should have stayed away from her, but I was young and reckless. I didn't learn my lesson quickly enough and was trying to find a way to make our relationship work despite all the issues between us. She was very bipolar. Sometimes, it was all good and everything was wonderful, and other times, the sky was falling, and it was obviously all my fault and I had to pay. Right before the event, she got upset because I was getting help from someone in the underground trance scene that she had a problem with. She was also suspicious of me trying to date other girls. Later, I found out that this was because she herself was constantly dating other guys behind my back. I don't remember why she got upset, but when it happened, she decided to confront me at my friend's place of business. He had a glass blowing studio at the time.

We were talking in her car, and she became aggressive. She stole my phone, thinking I was hiding some kind of betrayal. I can honestly say that I was not cheating on her or doing anything inappropriate. She, however, was totally convinced and probably still is. She got so upset that she started trying to break my phone in half, so I tried to take my phone back from her. It was at this point she pepper-sprayed me in her car, but in the commotion, she ended up spraying herself in the face. She let go of my phone and started pleading for a resolution. She let me out of the car, and I tried to recover. I went inside and yelled for someone to come outside to witness her mania. Only one person came out to help me, and it wasn't even someone I would have called a close friend at the time. When I came back outside, she had recovered and regained her anger, so she unloaded the entire can of pepper spray on me. I was wearing some cheap sunglasses, and thankfully, they completely protected my eyes somehow, but she soaked my head and back. It gave me a rash that felt like a sunburn. She drove off promising to get revenge on me, so I decided it was best that I didn't go home. She called me later that day claiming to be at my condo with the police, but I don't know if that was true or not. I was able to stay away from my place that day, but the event was in four days, so I talked to another friend who let me come and shower at their place right away to try and recover from the attack. I stayed at various friends' houses and worked on the event all the way up to the time the doors opened. There were sleepless nights. Numerous people contributed to make it possible. There were a few days of smaller private gatherings, where we took in the competition entries and then distributed them. This went well, but it was stressful, and there were a couple of problems that, luckily, were resolved. When everyone arrived at the venue, no one knew what was going to happen.

The event went well, considering the last-minute additions and ticket sales. Quite simply, it was pandemonium. There was a point where we had to stop selling tickets because it was obviously going to be oversold. We hoped that people would spread out their attendance enough to make it work. It was rough, and we played the game well, not releasing the venue location until the day of the event. There was some fear that an event with sales like we had arranged would not be allowed to go ahead once the local authorities found out. At the time, there was no permit you could apply for. We got everything we needed for a normal party of this nature, but we were still very much aware of the fact that there were things outside of our control. That being said, no one could have anticipated what happened.

It was getting close to the main portion of the evening with the major musical acts. People were having their minds blown. We had live glass blowing in the back, artists doing live painting in the front, 3D black light painting from a local graffiti artist, and all kinds of different booths representing the different aspects of cannabis culture. There were numerous glass blowers and distributors, rave companies, clothing companies and equipment companies for various cannabis productions. There were edible companies, seed companies, growers and hash vendors. We had a magician named Smoothini walking around the event performing tricks. (Later, he was on one of those huge talent competitions on TV.) A big group called The Great Glob Society showed up en masse; their fearless leader had done exceptionally well in the ticket sales competition and had won a booth. We had a VIP area, where anyone could try the entries from the competition. The event was supposed to go on until late, but just as the main artists were starting to perform, I got called to the front of the venue. There was a problem.

As I walked into the entrance area, I was met by 12 police officers in full riot gear. They were slightly overwhelmed, and they seemed to know they were responding to a call that was false. Someone — I think we all know who at this point — had called in a "rape in progress," and they needed to do a walk-through of the event. One guy actually had a plexiglass shield like you see on TV. They all had pads and head gear, and I'm not sure whether they had weapons. I was really nervous about the reaction people would have if they walked in like this unannounced. I was able to get the police to agree to wait at the front while we made an on-stage announcement, and I began telling the vendors as I was on my way back. A couple of them were very helpful and went to the stage to make the announcement while I went to the back room to inform everyone who was selling cannabis products. I could barely get back there it was so packed. Returning to the front, I could hear people saying the police were coming in before I had returned to give them the go-ahead. From what I was told, complete panic set in with the vendors. Some of them tossed all their hash and cannabis, collected their stuff and dipped out the back of the building.

It was now total chaos, with hundreds of people flooding into the streets, and the owners of the venue were forced to take the police around the areas that were not open to the party. I felt like I was having a heart attack the whole time. Part of me was thinking I would need to face the music once they saw the cannabis stuff. It was routine for cannabis prosecution to be much worse than more serious crimes, so I was expecting the worst. I was able to find the police and follow them as they walked out of the building, and they did absolutely nothing to anyone from what I saw. In fact, I never heard about them going after anyone on the street or anywhere else. As I walked out with them, one officer stayed behind the others. I could tell he was trying to get away from them so he could talk to me. He turned to me as they were leaving and asked, "Do you have any wax?" I could tell he was asking for himself and didn't want the other officers to know, but I couldn't take any chances, so I told him that I did not, and they all got in their cars and drove away. Hundreds of people had been scared off, but there were still hundreds of people who stayed to finish the party. We sped up the schedule and moved some things around so we could announce the awards and give the winners their trophies. The last performers got up and pumped it out so we could close it all down early. The event has gone down in cannabis history.

I thought it was all behind me. No other events were planned, and I wasn't thinking about doing another one after such a crazy experience. However, there's something about doing things that generate so much passion and excitement, and it was not long before the future looked different to me.

CHAPTER 10
OTHER SMALL PROBLEMS

osting wasn't supposed to be my responsibility, and the next few events led me to more problems. I was brought in as the event dates came closer because Big D was not confident the local people would be able to pull them off. Like me, various people had approached D and told him they wanted to host events in their local areas. In reality, not everyone was willing to really put in the time and effort or take the appropriate risks to make this happen. As I learned more about the details of each event, certain problems became evident, and the local hosts and I had to put in work to make them happen properly. Some issues were worse than others.

Washington state was first up, and this was probably the best of the bunch. The person who had taken this event on really wanted to work hard and do it right. They had (mostly) done what they needed to do, and there were only a couple of details that needed improvement. The general plan was to have a house or a local establishment where people would meet for the intake and competition portion of the event. This would usually also be the place where we would host our VIP pre-party. We then needed a large venue for the award show. This was sometimes moved around a little, depending on the details of the location and the state.

In Seattle, we had a local house in a great location, and the venue for the awards was the huge studio of a well-known glass blower who had offered to host the event. Issues arose when arranging food for the VIP party, but it all worked out in the end and was great. This was a really great example of how all the events could go in the future; it showed that the quality of the hosting efforts helped determine how successful events can be. The host had done a great job for this show but wasn't particularly experienced in hosting this kind of party. The issue we had with food was not difficult to overcome, and I identified it as a common problem. With my assistance, everything went well. The next event, however, would prove to be more difficult.

CHAPTER 11
LOSING VENUES AND MAKING THINGS WORK

The person hosting the Bay Area event had not done what they needed to do, and as a result, problems began to mount right away. Some things were coming together well. There was a very nice local house that we ended up renting last minute. We used it for all the competition-related events as well as the VIP party. The food for the VIP party was an issue again, but we found a local restaurant that could make enough empanadas for our party. They showed up with the biggest takeout order I've ever placed, and the food was delicious.

Prior to the event, we had identified issues with the original venue. I don't recall all the details, but most of the problems with venues usually boiled down to two things. Either the person who arranged the venue had not discussed the cannabis aspect of our event, or they had not properly measured the space to get an exact layout for selling the vendor booths. These two problems could result in absolute chaos. Obviously, the venues could cancel the event once they found out about the cannabis, either prior to or during the event. Additionally, the venue could be oversold for vendor booths. In the Bay Area, we had to bring in another person at the very last minute to secure a venue. The original host found a location that became impossible to use for the event, most likely for one of the above reasons, but I can't exactly recall. I never even saw the original venue, but thankfully, a last-minute location was sorted. It was so last minute, that I did not get to see it until moments before the show.

This location was fine with cannabis and smoking, but no one had measured it properly. It was generally used for underground parties with almost no booths. Right away, I realized the size was a huge problem. As we were placing the first vendors, we had to design a new layout because there was no way to fit everyone with the booth sizes they had initially signed up for. I had to apologetically explain the situation to each vendor and see if they were willing to squeeze into a smaller booth for the price they already paid, or if they wanted a refund. It ended up working out. Enough canceled and took the refund to make room for the people who wanted to stay. There also wasn't too much confrontation; most people reluctantly accepted the situation and rolled with it. Unfortunately, many people were disappointed in this event, including me. A part of me was truly happy when it was over.

CHAPTER 12
PROBLEM SOLVING FROM PLACE TO PLACE

C olorado had played host for the first event, but by the second one, we had far outgrown the original venue. As more events took place and more people became aware of what we were doing, it became increasingly difficult to find a space willing to host the now not-so-Secret Cup. Other larger events were experiencing problems that had become public. This didn't help either. The place we used in Colorado the second time was previously used for another large event, and we were able to use this tactic to secure venues in other cities. The next few years would present us with many challenges.

As the Secret Cup expanded, we included the East Coast, international cities that were already famous for cannabis, and even some conservative places where the laws seemed more likely to create a problem. The event planning was no longer rushed, and we learned to work efficiently. However, we didn't have much money. Cannabis was becoming even more popular on the West Coast and in Colorado, but the East Coast and other countries we checked out were largely behind. There was definitely pressure for us to host in these locations, but with the cannabis laws and culture in these regions, it was becoming increasingly difficult for us to guarantee people's safety.

Fully aware of the difficult roads ahead, we decided to keep moving forward. This didn't eliminate any of the points of conflict, so we still frequently had to rely on last-minute problem-solving to make events work. These events had been such great experiences, and so many people wanted them in their hometowns, but we would even run into issues at places where we had previously hosted events. From place to place, there were stories that became part of the adventure; some were glorious, but the most popular tales were always the bad experiences.

In Washington, we were able to use the same location for the award show and for the house where people stayed. One night, we went out to enjoy the city, and they were building a beer festival on the streets around the house. By the time we got back, there were huge fences keeping us from returning to our beds. We talked to some security guards who were roaming around the fence line and politely asked if we could gain access to the house. They wouldn't let us through, even with one of them as an escort. Upset, I caused a bit of a ruckus, and they called supervisors over, who also wouldn't let us by. After some nasty words, we decided we could probably jump the fence and get back to the house, so we left them and walked down an alley. I jumped the fence and let the others in. We saw those security guards looking for us all night long. They were so upset by the things I had said to them about their miserable lives that they were on a mission to hunt us down, but they never did find us, and it was funny hearing their frustrations from safely inside the house.

Around that time, we hosted another Los Angeles competition. It went very well for the most part, and it was our all-time largest event. The previous venue problems had me on a mission to find a really good place, and I was able to find a production studio with multiple warehouses. The studio was completely open to our goals. They were used to film and TV projects that essentially did whatever they wanted. This was a valuable lesson that I learned to use in the future. Some of the TV shows they had hosted were big-name shows, like "America's Next Top Model" and various Disney productions. There was some strange stuff about the location to a degree, no other businesses like this near by and even some apartments, but for the most part it was an awesome venue. Because we had permission to use the outside area, we could really make it big.

Our biggest problem that year was the after-party. The shuttle service we hired was very easygoing, but we couldn't find a location with decent, affordable parking to do pickups and drop-offs. This called for an unusual solution. I had been to many house parties in my youth where street parking was used for multiple blocks, and so, we gambled on a chance that the laws would be in our favor. A friend lived nearby, and we simply made the shuttles pick up and drop off from this address, in the middle of a residential neighborhood. The friend told me people started parking in the neighborhood and lining up on the sidewalk in front of their home, and that the line became rather large. Police came to take a look at some point, but nothing happened from what I was told. The venue address was eventually given out and people started trying to drive directly to park. This resulted in numerous vehicles being towed away at the vehicle owners' expense. Loads of stoners were upset by this.

The other problem was the party itself. The person who was supposed to be the host couldn't promote it the way that they needed to, so in the end, we covered debts for them we shouldn't have had to cover. The event was a really strange mix. It had an underground party vibe that involved lots of special effects and decorations, but the host hadn't considered the nature of our event, or what would appeal to our attendees, so it flopped. They had purchased a ton of alcohol, thinking this would be the way to make money to pay for everything, but the event wasn't targeted toward people who drink. It was targeted toward people who enjoy psychedelic experiences, and anyone into that knows that drinking is usually not a big part of enjoying that mindset. The host ditched out on the bill and never paid us back for covering their losses. I wish they had ditched out before they did the party. They wouldn't have owed anything, and I could have thrown a much better celebration.

There was almost a fight during the award show between a couple of the vendors. One group went over to the other and made some inappropriate comments that were really upsetting. I was told about it and went to see what was going on. I made it known that I would need security to come to back me up. It got heated quickly, but the huge security guards were a helpful intimidation factor. Thankfully, cooler heads prevailed as they realized they would be tossed out and make no money if they didn't behave.

Prior to the first East Coast event, many of our friends were predicting the worst. The marijuana laws out West were different from the new medical marijuana regulations in various states all over the U.S., especially those in or around the East Coast. The crime in these areas was also a factor we had been warned about. Thankfully, we didn't experience this — for the most part. Authorities didn't give us any trouble, and no one was robbed or anything like that.

The event was a success mostly due to the main hosts and their efforts to make it the best it could be. However, one person who had been brought in to be a host did virtually nothing and became a real big problem. He was responsible for checking measurements and planning rentals, as well as other typical event promotion duties. He sent phone numbers for us to call, but nothing that really needed to be done was done, and we had to do much of it ourselves upon arrival and rely on other local people to step up and do his job. At one point, he started to understand how little he had contributed. Days before the event, he used some of his previous music experience to lock in a well-known hip-hop artist for a price we could actually afford. The only reason we could even pay for that was because of the efforts of other local hosts who made the event one of the biggest to date. He still expected to be paid more than them by the end of it all, because of his music contribution. This problem person was such a negative influence it created numerous issues for many of the other people involved with the event. This persisted after the event was over. He and a few others decided to try to damage our reputation and business. This may have been the partial cause of some of the problems that came back to hurt a few of the local people involved in the show. A few months after our show, the location we used had a fire, and all kinds of terrible details became evident. Unfortunately, many people faced prosecution in connection with that fire. My heart still goes out to them.

We did a couple of events in Las Vegas that really pushed the line too. The first was a Cup finals event, and we rented a mansion a few minutes from the strip. This event was featured in the documentary film "The Secret Cup" (which is available for free on YouTube and Tubi). Wild times, indeed. People realized things were going missing, and at some point, we discovered that the staff had secret ways of coming in and out of the property. They appeared to be drug addicts of the worst kind, and thieves. This was not to say that drugs were not being used at the house by people at the parties as well. In fact, we had a notorious incident one night that a friend of mine brought to my attention right before everything went really badly. Earlier in the night, I had been in front of the house, welcoming people to the party. At some point, a person I didn't know well was telling me he had come with another person. This other person was well-known in the community for his hand-painted hats. This guy asked me if I had seen his artist friend, and when I said that I hadn't, he made a comment to the effect of "I hope he doesn't get into trouble." I was worried I might have to deal with this guy getting out of hand, getting sick or doing something unexpected, but I decided to blow it off. Toward the end of the night, my friend approached me and was visibly upset.

I was distracted and knew he had been partying, so I wasn't expecting what he told me. Apparently, he had been in my room, which had essentially hosted the staff party, providing a space for people to get away from the crowds. There was a girl in there with him, and she had her dog with her. The hat guy had entered and started getting uncomfortably close to the girl, calling her his girl-friend's name and saying some pretty terrible sexually suggestive stuff while backing her into a corner. My friend said he had to get involved. The hat guy seemed to be really messed up on something or a mixture of things. By the time my friend got to me, the hat guy had disappeared, so I went looking for him. Opening the door to one of the bedrooms, I saw him lying on the bed with his pants down. He was not aroused, but he was furiously masturbating. He looked directly at me with dead eyes as if he didn't know me. I screamed something to the effect of "What the fuck are you doing?!" and slammed the door. I took off to look for his friend. I told him there was a problem and that we needed to go back and get the hat guy from the room. We were too late, of course.

While I was gone, the hat guy must have gotten scared. I only know what happened from the stories that went around. Apparently, he came out of the room (still not wearing pants) and started to head for the door. My room was at the front of the house at the top of a sprawling spiral staircase, which was like something out of a Disney movie. The room he was in was across the hallway. When he came out of the room, he was standing at the top of the stairs in full view of around 100 people in the large room below. One by one, they started to notice him, and he walked down the stairs toward the front door. Some screamed, some made shocked gasps and others pointed and laughed. He got scared again, but at this point, he was not close enough to any of the doors to go back. If I recall correctly, he was still holding his penis. He decided to make a break for a bathroom that was down a hallway just a few steps from the bottom of the stairs. He somehow made it in there, and a huge crowd formed outside the bathroom. This is when I arrived at the scene with his friend.

His friend was essentially useless. Thankfully, one of the people at the party, who was a regular at our events, took responsibility for possibly enabling this situation and did his best to try and help the guy. I made an effort to stop people from taking pictures. It was really an awful scene. I was ready to violently remove the guy I was so upset. Big D managed to calm me down, and eventually, the hat guy was moved from the bathroom to the back guest house and taken care of by his friend and some other people. I had to be talked into allowing this rather than throwing him in a taxi and sending him somewhere else. It ended up being the better decision, so I am glad I went along with it. The event was so full of good times that even this became a hilarious story that made it more of a positive experience for many of the attendees. The girl wasn't harmed, and to my knowledge, nothing truly bad ever came of it for anyone. All of the people involved rolled with the weirdness and were cool about it. I don't think the guy even got called out about it publicly very much.

Some of the other house guests at the event were not so wonderful, but I won't throw them under the bus even though I probably could. We heard stories of potential legal problems, but no authorities ever came to shut anything down. This was extremely fortunate because the last few days of the event ended up getting out of hand in terms of cars and people. We were very, very lucky. I had been told that we were "protected" by someone I knew and that we narrowly dodged a bullet. I was never able to confirm or deny that. Good times.

At some point after the first East Coast event, we were approached by some locals to do a New England event. We really loved working on the East Coast and wanted to go back and do more, so we started putting it together. This time, we didn't have the same support as we had had for the first event for what seemed like trivial reasons. It really is unfortunate how intertwined business is with personalities, and how ego-driven some people are. This may have been the issue this time around, because we ended up hosting a very small event compared to what it could have been. Things went well enough for the most part. However, as the award show began, there were whispers of more problems.

The location we were using had been having issues with local authorities, and there were debates over the legality of the establishment. This first came to my attention when I observed some talk between the owners and the staff that seemed secretive. I watched them talking, and they kept going back and forth to the window. I kept an eye on them, and I could tell something was up, but I was also used to this by now. I decided to let it play out before getting too involved or getting worried. As time progressed, it wasn't looking any better, so I asked what was going on. They told me they thought a suspicious van parked in an adjacent lot was potentially the authorities and that they may be surveilling the event. They were a little worried, but they figured the authorities were likely after the property owner. At some point, he decided it would be best for him to visibly leave the event and go home. Him leaving seemed to do the trick. Nothing happened, and we concluded the event and award show as planned.

A couple of events that we threw did end up getting shut down. We hosted an event with a person from Washington, D.C., who really supported the competition and was a regular participant in them. This was a tough one to organize as it was in a city where the scene was not as large as it was in many of the other places we had gone. At the same time, I thoroughly enjoyed the experience. We had great hosts, and for once, we had time to properly enjoy the local attractions. The event was hosted entirely by the locals. They just used our name so that they could maximize the potential profits and we could reduce our expenses. The award show was going really well, but toward the end of the night, there was a commotion. Something bad had happened outside.

At the door, security guards and staff were taking tickets and carrying out normal entry attendance duties. A guy came running up to the door of the venue and told them he had been robbed for his shoes around the corner from the entrance. The story was strange, but he was barefoot and did seem shaken by the experience. I wasn't told if he was an event attendee or not. Shortly after this, the police showed up. They were there because a shooting had happened very close by the entrance. I figured this might be related to the other incident. They were not really concerned with the event, and even let it continue for a while, but eventually shut down the party early. It was a good experience, but also a scary one. There was even a point where I thought my rental car had been stolen. I had never realized how drastic the class separation was in Washington, D.C. It was glaringly obvious, and I really feel for the people involved in that struggle.

CHAPTER 13
TALKING TO DETECTIVES IN COLORADO

We put on so many events across the United States and even went to places like Spain and Amsterdam. It really was a big adventure. Certain places presented minor problems, like the ones described in the last chapter, but others posed more serious threats, making our jobs much more difficult. Places you'd assume would welcome marijuana often responded in a really destructive manner. The industry leaders tended to be self-serving.

Calaveras County, in California, revealed in a community announcement that local cannabis businesses were not supporting our event. Vendors informed us about this announcement, passing along warnings of law enforcement involvement. This drastically impacted attendance and really hurt everyone involved, especially the local businesses that did participate.

In Santa Cruz, California, several local businesses in the cannabis industry didn't want us to put on an event. In fact, they legally forced the venue to cancel after we had already booked with them and started promoting. We couldn't find another venue in town willing to have us, so we had to move to a different city. Various establishments felt threatened by the fact we had the absolute best companies from around the world participating in our shows. They were worried that they might lose business when their customers saw that they were paying too much to local providers. In reality, these providers only cared about making the most profit they could and preventing competition from developing. Sadly, we saw this repeatedly in emerging industries across various cities all over the world.

One of these places was Colorado. Colorado was where the event had first started, and where the laws surrounding cannabis were improving the most. Legislation was becoming less vague. In some ways, laws were moving toward legalization, but there were also more and more ways for a person to be considered in violation of these laws. The new rules and regulations were becoming increasingly restrictive, while cannabis seemingly moved into the mainstream. This meant that there was less danger for consumers and some businesses. Our last event in Colorado really brought this to light.

The first event was a "Wild West" experience. Nobody really knew what to expect, but we hoped for the best, and at the time, there simply wasn't enough exposure for authorities to become overly concerned. This carried over to the next couple events, and the worst issues we experienced were rain and snow that brought about flooding and parking drama. The community in Colorado had substantially grown over the years, and the city of Denver had become much more aware of the cannabis industry and the many factors involved. Our event was not the only game in town. Many smaller and more reckless events had occurred, and because of these, there was a lot of negative exposure. The growth of the community was both a blessing and a curse. We had more sponsors and vendors that wanted in, as well as more competitors, but the local authorities were also becoming more proactive in their attempts to prevent cannabis events that involved smoking and vending. This required some creative planning, specifically with regard to the award show, which, of course, didn't go quite the way we thought it would.

When I arrived in Colorado, I learned that we would be working with an event company that would be hosting. From the get-go, I was worried. Not because of the authorities, but because of the colossal bill the event company presented us with. I had been used to doing everything myself. While my approach involved more work, it was also much less expensive. This company had arranged both a local bar/restaurant, with a large outdoor area for the award ceremony, and an alternative location — their very own parking lot, where they kept all their event equipment rentals and supplies. This seemed fine to me, but as usual, I needed to visit the location to map out the vendor booths. The size of the bill didn't really make sense if we were only going to be using an empty parking lot.

There were many discussions about how we could save money, and the company was really trying to work with us. Maybe they thought it would be worthwhile someday.

Hosting the event in the parking lot was an attempt to save both time and money. This was the larger of the two locations, so there would be no issues with overbooking our vendors. We had used similar locations in other states, and the events had gone well, so it was not too bad of an idea at first. Soon after discussing it, we were informed that other tenants in the area had expressed their disapproval of a cannabis event being hosted there. Because of this, we were asked to use the other location. This would be a bit more risky, as the permits had been filed openly and included the name of the event. This meant it was impossible for us to be discreet. The location was small, but we had no other options. We had to give it a go.

Our event was scheduled between two larger events, the High Times Cannabis Cup and the Gypsy Jane Festival. Both had very similar concepts. They had huge price tags and boasted vendor booths and big concerts. The High Times crew was very experienced and had hosted some large events, possibly the largest of this kind. Gypsy Jane was not experienced at all and was working off the theory that a cannabis festival with music all day — in addition to games, entertainment and standard vendor booths — would be hugely successful now that legalization made it possible to smoke without a medical card. Spoiler alert: It ended up being a big mistake, and according to my friend, who worked as their cannabis expert, they lost about $900,000.

It turned out that the same company that we were using for our event production was also working with the Gypsy Jane festival and had lots of prior experience with mainstream events. They had made some interesting plans, and now, we could put them to the test.

First, we needed to check out the new venue. I arrived at the location with the representatives from the event promotion company, and we began our walk-through. The area was small and exposed, but it looked like it could work. We walked around for a bit and discussed how we would set up privacy fences. As usual, cost effectiveness was the priority. It wasn't long before we noticed that some of the people at the venue were not part of our event. They were trying to remain incognito, but I was quickly informed as to who they actually were.

Two gentlemen were having a discussion with the owner of the bar/restaurant. They were detectives, and I later discovered they were telling the owner that if he went forward with the event then they would take away his alcohol license. At first, I was a bit afraid, but after thinking about my options, it became clear that I needed to talk to them. We didn't want to take any unnecessary risks, for the sake of both our vendors and the attendees. The detectives were told that the promoter of the event was there, and I sent word that I wanted to talk to them about their issues with the event.

The detectives took us to a quiet place to talk where nobody else could hear what we were talking about or, more importantly, what threats they were going to make. I asked what the problem was, and they said that their main issue was people smoking cannabis in a semi-public place. It was all cordial at first, and they said they were not going to stop us from putting on the event, but they would be there to issue infractions. I was very polite, asking questions about how we could proceed without any violations. They argued that these events were illegal and that there was essentially no way to do them legally. They were not receptive to my questions about removing vending and remedying any other issues they seemed to have. They became combative, as I was rebutting their statements, but they were trying to be vague as well, eventually saying, "You guys all act like we are stupid, but we know everything that is going on, and we will issue citations and enforce the full extent of the law." That really bothered me. It seemed like we were being singled out. Then things got even more confusing.

They had stopped being nice and had become flustered and emotional. It seemed like they were not entirely confident of their legal standing on these issues, but clearly wanted to stop the event nonetheless. So I asked them how the High Times event had occurred just a week or two prior, and they became very evasive. They acted like they didn't know what I was talking about. Then I really upset them. I said, "You just told me that you know everything that's going on. Yet now, you're pretending to act like you don't know about the event I'm talking about — that had over 40,000 people in attendance — just a few days ago." They were angry with me and stated that the other event was not in their jurisdiction and that they couldn't tell me anything about that, but that our event would certainly result in arrests.

They went to leave, but I wasn't about to let them go so easy. I began referencing medical laws and the fact that patients needed to be able to consume their medicine when they were not at home. They repeated that smoking cannabis in public was a violation of the law and that they would be issuing citations to anyone in the area doing so, both at the venue and outside of it. They again said there was no legal way to host the event, and while they couldn't stop us from moving forward, they would enforce the law to the fullest extent possible. They had no intention of trying to work with us to make it safe for everyone involved. They then stormed off with condescending farewells.

It was at this point that we discussed moving to another city, and we turned to our community to find an answer. There were a couple of locations that were essentially next door, in the city of Colorado Springs, but that was over an hour away from the previous location. As we negotiated the terms, we also had to let everyone know the new details. Vendors, sponsors and attendees all had to be informed. We were going to honor refunds and offer alternatives for anyone who was upset or simply not able to make these changes work. Our glass blower demo was an issue, but the artists were very supportive, and most came through to find a way to make it work. Some vendors had to pull out, and others decided to hold out for future events. Our music artists were all very cool about it. We got them new hotels, and it was a real group effort to smooth it out. It seemed like everything that could go wrong already had, but — big surprise — there was one last incident.

I had parked our rental car out front on the street, where a few other cars were already parked. As we were setting up, I remember hearing a big crashing sound. A young kid who had likely been out partying lost control of his vehicle. He plowed into a few cars, and the last one had someone sitting inside of it! Thankfully, nobody was seriously injured. Of course, he hit my rental as well. The damage was so bad that he totaled all three of the cars he hit. One of my most reliable staff members dealt with this while I tried to arrange the vendors and plot out the layout of the venue. The police came to handle the situation with the kid and the damaged vehicles — and were not concerned with our event. In the end, the event was a success. After that experience, we had a team meeting and decided that because the changing laws were no longer working in our favor, we would avoid doing any events in Colorado until things improved. They never did get any better. In fact, they got much worse over the following years.

One of the most terrible things about the illusion of legalization was that things we had thought were harmless and wonderful had become demonized and targeted. The physical appearance and general filthiness of many historically outspoken cannabis advocates was now becoming a problem for businesses, and individual complaints rose as these "wooks," as they are often called, openly spent time in central parts of the city, unafraid of arrest. This was not going to be the last time that targeted persecution of this kind ruined an event like ours. Honestly, it was one of the worst times for many people in the community; we were realizing that the efforts we made and risks we had taken were not going to pay off the way we had thought. Instead, our efforts had led us to some of the most awful situations and were being used against us.

CHAPTER 14
SHUT IT DOWN
OR GET ARRESTED

The second time we went to Arizona was probably my closest call to actually getting arrested while hosting The Secret Cup events. This was because of my prior history with the state.

Arizona already held some bad experiences for me because of a prior arrest, and I was somewhat concerned about going back there. Even though my case had been over for a while, the attorney had told me they had something like seven years to charge me again if they could find probable cause. They were clearly not happy that there was nothing they could do to me the last time around. It was entirely plausible that they were waiting for me to make the mistake of coming back to the state.

My visit for the first Arizona Secret Cup went surprisingly well. We had a good group of people who had chosen the location, and everything went about as well as it could have for a first show. Scheduling a second event seemed like a good idea.

What I didn't know was that there had been smaller events going on at the same location during the year after our first event. The organizers had had problems with the authorities in relation to those events. Had I known, I would have chosen a different location, but I thought because the first time had gone so smoothly, that this location would be fine. Given the location, I probably should have been more cautious anyway.

The place was primarily used for wedding receptions and events of that nature. It was a decent size: They had a small parking lot and a large outdoor space where a medium-sized stage could be set up. Attendance would max out anywhere from 500 to 2,000 people, depending on the layout. There was also a good-sized indoor area. The red flag, however, was that it was right in the middle of a city, surrounded by regular stores like CVS and Walgreens. The likelihood of some random person walking by and seeing what was going on, or even just noticing the smell of marijuana, was likely. If they notified the authorities, it would be a problem for us — and that's essentially what happened.

Our first day went really well. We had a decent turnout and a ton of booths, almost double the number from the first event. The vendors seemed to be doing well enough, and there were no conflicts. Our glass demo was looking good, and everything was going smoothly, at least from our perspective. The second day, however, there was an issue. I'm not entirely sure if this person was around on the first day, and I'm not really sure what set them off, but I would assume it was the smell of pot. It can be really noticeable and can spread quite far, especially considering the quantities people consumed at our events.

I was called over to the ticket table where people check in, and they informed me of a person who had just come up to the table. This person didn't have a ticket and was asking questions about the event. I had instructed everyone to be honest, and so, they had told the guy what was going on. They said it was a medical marijuana event for people who have a medical recommendation from a doctor. He asked if he could buy a ticket, and they allegedly told him that he could if he had his recommendation. He was not happy and stormed off. Someone from the event followed him for quite a way down the street, where he eventually got into a car and drove away. I told everyone to just keep doing what they were doing, and there were no more problems until an hour or two later.

About four police SUVs showed up to the event, and the cops walked up to the ticket table, asking to speak to the event organizers. I knew that was me, but I went to find the local hosts to see where we were standing as far as permits. They told me they had not obtained any additional permits, other than the standard contracts for renting the venue. That meant that our outdoor music was probably a violation, and who knows what else. There was suddenly a mass exodus by anyone who had something to be concerned about. All those who had never experienced the police before were simply scared for their lives.

I went over to the ticket table and told the cops I was the one they were looking for. I did my best to smooth out the situation, but they were ready to arrest someone, so I knew I had to just take it easy and roll with the punches. The officer I was talking to quickly decided that it was time to call her higher-ranked officer in charge. The officers told me to wait with them at the front while they waited for him to arrive. Around this time, I gave the go-ahead for my team to start telling the vendors to pack up or, at the very least, make their booths as "legal" as possible in case anyone wanted to start looking around, as they had done at other events. I asked some questions and talked with the officer a bit. Someone recorded a video of all of this, which might still exist somewhere. It was difficult, partly because I was from California. Though I knew a little about Arizona laws, I didn't know enough to stand up for myself. I didn't know how much I could rightfully resist. Eventually, the officer in charge arrived and came my way.

Visibly upset, he started asking basic questions. I was as honest as I could be, but I knew I still should try to be as vague as possible. He wanted to know if people were smoking pot and what else was going on. I gave the basics, but I left out the details of what some of the booths were selling (i.e., cannabis products) and focused on the stuff like clothing and glass art. I could tell he wanted to arrest me, but when I told him I was from California, things changed. I think he was under the impression I was from Arizona and was connected to the events held at this location that they had previously had issues with. The conversation ended with him stating that he was going to return in about an hour, and if everything was not shut down by then, he would start arresting people.

That was all I needed to hear, and we shut down the event right away. This was the only event we ever had to shut down once it had already started, and it was a heartbreaker for everyone. Many of the vendors were upset. We couldn't even do the award ceremony, so a bunch of the competitors were upset as well. All in all, it was not really a big deal because nobody got into any serious trouble, and that was the most important thing. The awards were eventually distributed to the people who had won, and we announced the winners online so that everyone could see the results. Even so, it was awful.

Some amusing things happened after this incident. I had been standing with my arms behind my back, and someone had taken a picture of me. It looked like I was in cuffs. Some social media posts popped up, demanding my freedom. It was hilarious. #FreeRigRags.

Using this photo, one of my friends played a trick on some other friends who were not at the event. They told them I was arrested and asked me to play along. I had assumed he was going to tell them shortly after they had fallen for it, but no, he let them think I was arrested until the next day. They did not think it was funny, and that was funny in itself because they were the type of people who love trolling people.

CHAPTER 15
FESTIVAL DE CANNABIS & MILITARY POLICE

My most popular story about facing the strong arm of the law occurred in Spain.

Every year, for over a decade now, there is a seed convention in Spain called Spannabis. It started small but is now a really big event. At the time, the organizers wanted to expand by hosting a second event in a nearby city — Madrid. The original event was in Cornella de Llobregat, a small town near Barcelona. I had never been anywhere in Spain before, but I had been to Amsterdam probably ten times at this point, so I felt like I knew what Europe would be like.

We were obviously throwing a cannabis competition, but the whole dabbing scene in Europe was very different. In Amsterdam, because of stricter hash laws, there was not as big of a scene as most would think. In Spain, while there were strict laws about how cannabis clubs could operate, they did allow dabbing and sold hash concentrates that were dab-able. There were not many people making concentrates there, compared to the places we normally went in the United States, so we opened the competition up to include entrants from anywhere, and we encouraged other countries to enter. We had a couple of the biggest U.S. companies enter in Spain, and one of the regular competitors at our events wanted to compete at the last minute. He was a big supporter of ours, and had become a member of the fam, so I was motivated to help him. He talked me into taking his entry when we were on the plane.

I had been nervous the first few times I went to Amsterdam, but nobody ever said anything to me, so I got used to just getting my bags and walking out of the airport door like nothing was amiss. I had figured Spain would be the same, so I didn't stop to think about what I would be bringing with me this time.

One of the special things about our events were the prizes. Many companies were very generous with the items they made for us in return for promotional involvement. This event in particular had some amazing prizes. We had glass oil rig cups that were functional and gorgeous. Those came in gun cases. We had a few electronic nails (otherwise known as E-Nails) that looked a lot like explosives. There were also all kinds of smaller things, like medals. I needed to get a third suitcase to carry all of it, and I still barely had enough space. Inside one of the E-Nails, I may or may not have stashed the competitor's entry for the competition.

I flew to Spain without incident. As far as I knew, the whole way there, nothing was wrong. When we arrived, and I got my carry-on bag, I didn't notice anything strange until I was about to step out into the jetway. There was a military police officer standing at the door, and the airline attendants were communicating with him in Spanish. He had something in his hand, along with his machine gun. It was my picture. It looked like a photocopy of my passport. He spoke to me in English: Everything was fine, there was nothing to worry about, but I needed to come with him.

I immediately knew everything was not fine, and I figured I was in some kind of trouble, but I also knew it was best I keep my cool. So I gathered myself as best as I could. I get fairly sick flying, so I was uncomfortable already. As he escorted me through the airport, he repeatedly told me that everything was fine, no big deal, but I needed to come with him. I got the feeling he was worried I would run. I wasn't thinking about doing that, but I did keep asking him if he could tell me anything more about what this was about. Nope, just that I was not to worry.

We eventually reached an underground area of the airport, and a bunch of military-looking police officers were there. He took me to a table where all my suitcases were sitting out. They were open, but nobody had gone through them yet. They told me that they needed permission to search my bags, so I told them to go ahead. I honestly didn't know what to do, but I thought if I resisted, it would probably be much worse. They proceeded to go through each of the bags. The first one was all my personal stuff, so there was nothing of interest for them in there, and they blew by it. The second big bag was the prizes and trophies. The smaller third bag had a mix of random stuff.

As they were going through the second bag, someone else started looking through the third bag with the prizes in it. They were pulling out the gun cases and opening them up to see the glass bongs inside. The officers kept pulling things out of the case and looking at the boxes with puzzled faces. They were joking with each other a little, but all in Spanish. At that point, they weren't being particularly thorough, like U.S. police would be. I was just watching them and trying to contain the mini heart attack I was having. Just as I was starting to get really concerned, I heard them mention "Festival de Cannabis" and "Cornella de Llobregat" — the location of Spannabis.

The police officer who spoke English turned to me and asked, "Are you here for the Festival de Cannabis in Cornella de Llobregat?" I realized my opportunity here and, rather than trying to explain the details of our event, said, "Yes, that's why I'm here." Then he asked me if I had any paperwork for the booth. I said I didn't know where it was, but I was sure I did somewhere. He said it was no problem, that he didn't need to see it. He asked me one last question: "Do you have any cannabis?" I said that I didn't. I told them that I knew I was bringing all of this other stuff with me and would likely get in trouble. They packed up my stuff, and once again, it seemed I had dodged a bullet. I proceeded to host one of the most beloved events ever. I must be honest, I got sick in Spain and there were some big misunderstandings. In order to be fair to the people involved I have to be vague here. Some really special moments were mixed in with really awful moments. However, all in all, it was a wonderful adventure. I met amazing people, got to experience some really unique things, and did all the touristy stuff too.

CHAPTER 16
NUMEROUS PATROL CARS AND K9 UNITS

I n California, we hosted a few events in the northern part of the state. Our experiences here often differ from what most would expect. Southern California is known for the consumption of cannabis, but Northern California is known for the cultivation of cannabis. Many people think it is much less strict up north, but that really isn't the case. In fact, because the authorities are more familiar with how people break the laws to grow cannabis, they can often be more assertive in many ways. They can be more under-standing, too, don't get me wrong, but there are some laws that are different from the top of the state to the bottom. In many ways, California is not the marijuana paradise that outsiders assume it is.

The events in NorCal have been some of my personal favorites. Others came close, but the ones up there were all really special. I think of those times often and fondly. (I haven't talked about the good things much in this book. Maybe I'll write a follow-up about all the great times and crazy adventures.) The camping events were a special kind of wonderful, and the ones we had on the East Coast — even those plagued by rain — were amazing too. As fantastic as those events were, they all had their problems.

The first one we were doing, in Mendocino, started out as expected. We couldn't find a location in the Bay Area that suited our needs and our budget, or one that was willing to do another cannabis event after hosting other larger shows. Normally, I needed a local person familiar with the city to help with planning, but we didn't fill this role for this event. Some of these people had really made planning more difficult in the past, so I was on my own. I had a few venues recommended to me, and I contacted them all, but nothing was viable until I got a return call out of the blue.

Early in the planning process, I had talked to someone who suggested doing the event in the real NorCal. They said they worked at a venue that might work. The problem was that the owner was not going to be around for a while. I explored some other options during that time, but all my efforts reached dead ends. When the owner got back, they approved of the concept, called me and saved the day. I went up there right away to see the venue. It was going to be more than adequate for the vendors and for what we had planned. We were also able to do a really special glass blowing demo there. Unfortunately, in the end, we didn't do well financially.

That first camping trip was a concept that came to be out of necessity—we couldn't find a venue; we had not made an effort to plan it. The owner and his team not only saved us from canceling our NorCal event but also led us to the new concept. There were a bunch of problems that weekend that we managed to smooth over, setting the tone for our NorCal experiences. Thankfully, I was educated about the laws regarding concentrates in that region, but they were much stricter than the rules we had in SoCal.

The next event's location was introduced to us by some of the people who worked on the first camping event. This time, we would be in Humboldt County, the "home" of California cannabis, in a city called Trinidad. The event site was in the middle of a huge redwood forest. The property had a restaurant and bar; cabins and amenities; a supermarket and beach within walking distance; and enough space to accommodate everything we had planned. It was one of the most perfect locations I had ever seen.

Now for the scary part.

I drove up from the Hollywood area in SoCal, where I lived at the time. We had hosted the intake for the competition at an alternative location about a week before. Some of the people who entered didn't want to drive a few hours north for the camping event, so they got their kit early, and we tried to make it work for everyone. After everything was arranged and blindly relabeled, we had close to 35 competitors and something like 40 official kits. These had to be brought up to the event to be distributed to the rest of the judges/ competitors, so I put them in my car and headed up north with them.

I was driving with two friends who had never been to the location before. I was familiar with this drive and that it could take a really, really long time if you were not extremely punctual with your stops. I was driving with all these judge kits, and regardless of the location, these were not something you would want to get caught with. I was trying to drive fast but smart and take no extra time. My passengers were drinking and partying while we drove the whole way up and around the Bay Area. They started needing to stop to go to the bathroom frequently. I was not being very understanding of this, and at one point, they wandered off to a market during one of the stops. I was so angry. I went and got food for myself and then came back to find them. We lost a bunch of time. Now, because of this, we were going to be late to an event I was supposed to be hosting.

I started driving much faster so we could get up there before 3 a.m. It was a long drive, and I was making good time, but somewhere around Garberville, we ran into a problem. I was driving too fast, and in my rearview mirror, I noticed what looked like a cop car. I slowed down a bit, and as I did, they put on their lights to pull me over. I was really worried. (I think all these experiences have contributed to something like a PTSD reaction that I still suffer from today when dealing with the police.) I told myself it was probably just a speeding ticket. I just wanted to get it over with and move on.

As the cop came up to the passenger side, he told me I was speeding, and he started peeking around the car. I thought we were at least smart enough to have not left out anything obvious, and I hadn't picked up on any noticeable smell. He shined his flashlight on a brand-new little pipe my friend had shown us earlier. He had made it himself, and it was sitting in the cup holder. The pipe was totally clean, but now, of course, I knew the cop had a reason to search the car if he wanted to. The officer went back to his car for a while, and I really started sweating. I was terrified he was going to search the car and find the judge kits and everything else we had. Eventually, he came back to my window and said that I needed to slow down. I signed the speeding ticket.

We were so lucky. I am not sure why we didn't get searched or hassled. He seemed like he was either new or nervous. Whatever the reason may have been, we had dodged yet another bullet. The event went exceptionally well. In fact, this was probably the most special event that I ever threw. Of course, I wanted to come back again the next year. By then, even more people would know about us. However, it turned out that not everyone would receive such a warm welcome.

The previous year had been a great event, but we wanted to see if we could make a profit and include things that would make the event more fun. This meant adding to the marketing budget and trying out some other ideas. We attached a huge banner to a truck that drove around town and through nearby cities. This got the word out to many potential show-goers, but it also spread the word to the authorities. After talking with the property owner, I found out there was a potential issue with the parking situation they had arranged with a nearby casino. We wanted to be respectful to the local businesses, and as such, we arranged parking and a shuttle service close by to reduce the number of people parking in random places across the city. On the first night, the casino officially canceled the casino parking, claiming that they had been pressured by the local police.

I was not going to play that game, so I told the other organizers that we would have to do the best we could with on-site parking, and everyone else could park in the city the way they had done in the previous year. The first night went well, but there was a visible police presence down the street from the event. They would drive up and down the street, then park nearby and watch. They did this all day long, and the next day, they started doing the same thing with K9 units. I wasn't sure what to make of it. We had a good-sized staff, and the entire place was fenced in by temporary event fencing that we had paid extra for. After displaying their numerous K9 units, they decided to pull up on the show.

I am fairly certain this was the second night of the event, but it might have been the third night. The event was in full swing. We had nothing going on performance wise, but people were partying all over. The bar was full, and people were smoking everywhere. The police had about six or eight cars, and at least two were labeled as K9 units. Clearly, their plan was to search the whole property, and they came into the bar and started doing just that. I remember seeing them pull up, and hearing what was going on through a staff radio. I may or may not have taken LSD earlier in the night, so you can imagine what my mindset was like. I was about to go over and handle it, but the staff told me to let the property owner go. He had a better relationship with the local police than I did. This was fine by me, and I was happy to not have to be the one to deal with the issue.

There wasn't much that could be done, but he was able to stop them from entering the main areas of the event with the K9s, or go raid all the campers and cabins, or whatever their plan was. The staff had the back gate of the bar locked, and so, for some reason, the police could only search people in the bar up to that point. We were so lucky. They only got a few people in the bar from what I heard, and they left reluctantly. However, the police were angry. They went up the street and started pulling over all the cars that left the event that night. I heard they got some folks that way. This was enough for me to decide that it would be our last event at this location, for everyone's safety.

After so many close calls, this would turn out to be my last battle with police as an event host. I was happy to avoid the law one more time, but memories like these are bittersweet to me now that cannabis events are somewhat legal.

AFTERWORD

For the most part, my journey with cannabis has been a positive one. I watched as the community turned the industry into what it is today. My stories consist of good times, fantastic people and amazing adventures, and I've been able to talk about these wonderful experiences on many podcasts and in other media appearances. While I tend to emphasize the good side of my cannabis journey, people are usually more interested in the scary stories. I decided it would be a good idea for me to compile these bits of my history. In the future, I can simply tell people to go and read my book if they want to hear about my horror stories, rather than recount them over and over again. This also might be a better way to help more people.

I've learned so much from my various roles in the cannabis sphere: consumer, dealer, event organizer and host. I feel I found myself during these times. Cannabis went from being an illegal thing that only stoners and "degenerates" loved to a medicine that could help people. The changes in the way people perceived and used it were phenomenal. The way events in the United States started developing was exciting, and my time leading the charge was so special in many ways. I had the privilege of experiencing so much of cannabis culture, both in the States and internationally. I finally achieved the rock star lifestyle that I had always admired as a child. However, I was also part of a movement that was changing society.

I look back on these stories, good and bad, with gratitude. I wear them like badges of honor in the (ongoing) war against marijuana. Even as I am writing them now, I find myself thinking about how ridiculous most of these situations were. For the most part, it was all about persecution for consumption.

Look at the laws and the opportunities that came about when the conversation changed from "marijuana is medicine" to "marijuana is big money." States were lukewarm when marijuana was being portrayed as a medicinal plant with health benefits for many. Once people in states like Colorado and California started talking about the tons of cash they were making, more and more states began jumping on the bandwagon.

As advocates, we faced the total unfairness and harsh prosecution of the law and stood up for what we believed was the right thing. We saw the U.S., which used to be a place that loved marijuana but forced consumers to buy from back-alley dealers, become the home of legal cannabis. Before legality, the cannabis choices ranged from good expensive weed to bad cheap weed. In some ways, this may still be the case, but now, we have a remarkable diversity of strains, and we have a wealth of knowledge that was previously only part of cannabis culture in Amsterdam.

Today, people can be growers, hash makers, bud tenders or delivery drivers, and there are all kinds of other packaging/trimming/processing jobs. Some have their own companies with their own brands of cannabis products, and they advertise these items fairly openly. An end is in sight for marijuana prohibition, and even places outside of the U.S. have relaxed their laws on cannabis.

We are winning. In many ways, we have already won. Cannabis will not be illegal for the children of the future in the ways that it was for us. In many states, laws are becoming even more progressive than those in California. The future for cannabis is bright. Although there have been many disappointments, for the most part, we have taken a step in the right direction.

In the coming years, I hope stories like mine will become absurd and beyond belief to the average person.

I look forward to seeing what amazing new directions the young people of today take cannabis in. The industry is in its awkward teenage phase, but it's on the cusp of maturation. There will no doubt be some moronic and embarrassing occurrences along the way before the inspirational and empowering people of the next cannabis generation emerge. Don't be dissuaded by the clown-like characters, the fraudulent accomplishments and the shameless influencers of today. Rather, find those honest individuals that have true passion and no façade. These are the people who will take us to the Promised Land.

Someday, we won't have to be ashamed of the representation of cannabis in the media spotlight, because the one thing we will be able to depend on is the authentic beauty of this wonderful plant and the miracles it creates every day.

My journey has been a wonderful adventure, and I wouldn't trade it for anything.

When you see me, feel free to come and say hello!

If you ask me, "How are you?"

I'll say, "High ... how are you?"

You've read the scary stories, so why not help me make positive ones?

May the wind always be at your back and the sun upon your face. And may the wings of destiny carry you aloft to dance with the stars.

—George Jung, cannabis pioneer

ABOUT THE AUTHOR

Jeremy Norrie is a journalist, filmmaker, and cannabis industry pioneer. He was among the first reporters to cover Mixed Martial Arts; he was the first artesianal hash oil producer to win an international award for concentrate. He later created and hosted numerous competitions all over the USA & internationally. More recently Norrie has gained note as an award-winning director and producer of documentary films on a range of topics, from The Cannabis Cup to Bigfoot to health and social topics like mindfulness and animal welfare. This is his first book. For more information, please see TheSkyIsland.com.

ABOUT THE PUBLISHER

The Sager Group was founded in 1984. In 2012 it was chartered as a multimedia content brand, with the intent of empowering those who create art—an umbrella beneath which makers can pursue, and profit from, their craft directly, without gatekeepers. TSG publishes books; ministers to artists and provides modest grants; and produces documentary, feature, and commercial films. By harnessing the means of production, The Sager Group helps artists help themselves. For more information, please see TheSagerGroup.net.

MORE BOOKS FROM
THE SAGER GROUP

The Swamp: Deceit and Corruption in the CIA
An Elizabeth Petrov Thriller (Book 1)
by Jeff Grant

Chains of Nobility: Brotherhood of the Mamluks (Book 1-3)
by Brad Graft

Meeting Mozart: A Novel Drawn from the Secret
Diaries of Lorenzo Da Ponte
by Howard Jay Smith

Death Came Swiftly: A Novel About the Tay Bridge Disaster of 1879
by Bill Abrams

A Boy and His Dog in Hell: And Other Stories
by Mike Sager

The Deadliest Man Alive: Count Dante, The Mob
and the War for American Martial Arts
by Benji Feldheim

The Orphan's Daughter: A Novel
by Jan Cherubin

Lifeboat No. 8: Surviving the Titanic
by Elizabeth Kaye

The Pope of Pot: And Other True Stories of Marijuana and
Related High Jinks

by Mike Sager

See our entire library at TheSagerGroup.net

THE SAGER GROUP

Artifex Te Adiuva